D0200491

LEXICON OF
SAUCES & DIPS

Preparation • Taste • Use • Recipes

Kristiane Müller-Urban

REBO PUBLISHERS

Photographs: CMA Deutsche Butter: p. 20; Food Look, Köln: p. 8, 38, 134, 135, 143, 175, 178, 180, 184, 186, 188, 203, 208, 213, 264, 288; Food Look, New York, Peter Medilek: p. 87, 96, 100, 101, 102; Kalifornische Mandeln: p. 220, 244; Christian Kargl: p. 76, 97, 118, 131, 132, 145, 148, 166, 210, 227, 238, 239, 242, 249, 267, Kikkoman: p. 42; Knorr: p. 79, 104, 126, 215, 246; Peter Kölln KGaA, Köllnflockenwerke: p. 120, 207, 209, 245, 255, 262; Maggi: p. 12 above, 62, 65, 75, 105, 137, 157, 173, 241, 243; Meggle: p. 225; Mondamin: p. 14, 44, 71; Schwartau: p. 250, 253, 254, 261, 264, 266; Brigitte Sporrer/Alena Hrbková: p. 10, 11, 13, 17, 22, 23, 24, 27, 28, 31, 32, 33, 34, 35, 37, 47, 49, 50, 51, 56, 58, 61, 66, 67, 68, 69, 76, 77, 78, 80, 82, 83, 86, 90, 92, 93, 94, 97, 98, 107, 110, 111, 114, 116, 117, 123, 124, 125, 128, 130, 139, 144, 149, 150, 153, 154, 158, 160, 163, 166, 167, 170, 172, 174, 177, 182, 190, 192, 196, 198, 201, 211, 216, 219, 222, 224, 236, 241, 252, 256, 264, 270, 279, 293; Surig: 12 below, 55, 72, 99, 103, 106, 122, 127, 129, 146, 159, 161, 165, 168, 169, 204, 205, 228, 229, 230, 232, 234, 235, 237, 242, 258, 281; Zespri Gold Kiwifrucht: p. 108

Text: Kristiane Müller-Urban
Typesetting: AdAm Studio, Prague, The Czech Republic
Cover design: AdAm Studio, Prague, The Czech Republic

Translation: Eva Camrdová for Agentura Abandon, Prague, The Czech Republic
Proofreading: Emily Sands, Laura Grec, Eva Munk

ISBN 90 366 1697 2

Table of Contents

Introduction

How it began: From the first salty broth to delicate, flavorful sauce

After people discovered fire, good flavor and the nutritional value of meat and vegetables, they invented cooking. They began roasting, boiling and frying food. But the concept of sauce was still undiscovered. Vegetable and corn were boiled in water, meat and fish were roasted over a blazing fire or in big kettles. Our ancestors' diet was quite different from ours nowadays. The first people to put salty broth on their cooked food were the ancient Romans. The first sauce-like marinades were used mainly for covering an unpleasant taste, rather than for refining a meal. Salty broth sauce originated because meat was salted to preserve it over long periods.

A sauce for the Marquis de Béchamel

We owe the first delicious sauces, as well as the roots of true culinary art, to the French. Over time, cooks, especially in France, learned how to make sauces more and more delicate. *Roux*, a French word, was invented in France in the 17th century. A roux sauce often served to make a meal more nutritious. A pound of carrots in a heavy flour sauce is ample for four or more eaters and more filling than 1 lb carrots carmelized in butter and sugar. Even today, sauces made from flour are considered lighter and more refined in taste.

We are especially grateful to one particular Frenchman: the cook who first composed this fine sauce out of roux, spices and milk for his master, Marquis de Béchamel. The cooks at the French court named their new creations after their lords. Duxelles, for example, is a method of preparing mushrooms, shallots, wine and parsley devised by the Marquis d'Uxelles' cook.

MODERN COOKING OF SAUCES

The first tasty sauces were Béchamel sauces, made from milk and flour, brown sauces (*sauces brunes*), velvet sauces (*veluté*) made of roux and broth and of course the Hollandaise, thickened with egg yolk. They all originated in France. A sauce was now more than a mask for an unpleasant taste. It enriched meals and whetted appetites. Royal cooks competed to concoct new delicacies for their illustrious employers.

Every food, whether it is roast pork, a crisp goose, vegetables, a salad rich in vitamins or a juicy steak, is enhanced by a good sauce. Sauces may be light or dark, consist of cream or meat juice, vinegar and oil, puréed or chopped vegetables, herbs, cheeses, fruits, chocolate or spices. With fresh ingredients, interesting seasonings, a bit of imagination and our proven recipes, you can successfully create mouth-watering sauces, dips and salsas.

SPICES FOR A GOOD TASTE

Water, gravy or braise juice, vegetable broth or wine, vinegar and oil are all bases for a sauce. The sauce is refined with or thickened by cream, butter or egg yolk, flour or starch. The most essential spices are, of course, salt and pepper, perhaps a pinch of sugar and the rest is left to the cook's imagination.

For seasoning, all spices and herbs are suitable. A good lesson on sauce preparation will be helpful for those who have always thought cinnamon and aniseed belong only in winter holiday cuisine or that mustard only goes with a smoked sausage and jam is best on a breakfast roll. Don't feel discouraged if your sauce lacks the flavor you intended. Add a little tomato paste or ketchup, according to your taste, a little sweet or hot mustard, even some marmalade or jam, to the sauce. A spoon of rose-hip paste gives venison sauce a special savor. Orange jam, lemon jelly or English ginger jam refine sauces for poultry and veal. Grated lemon, lime or orange peel can whet the appetite as well. A piece of plain chocolate added to a roast gravy is an unforgettable sauce experience.

Look around for spice mixtures in supermarkets and health-food shops. You will find something here for every taste. For instance, an Indian Tandoori-spice mixture which helped many a "German" sauce is always highly appreciated. Other spice mixtures are perfect for Mexican, Caribbean, Italian, or American dishes as well as for all other meals. Gingerbread spice mixtures are outstanding for dessert sauces and often savory in a venison or beef sauce.

> **TIP**
>
> Soup vegetables, mushrooms, tomatoes and all the spices, except for bay, should always be added during the last 30 minutes of meal preparation. Only this way will they keep their aromas. Otherwise their fragrance would irreversibly disappear, along with the steam, over a longer period of cooking. Fresh herbs, except for thyme, rosemary and sage, should always be added to a finished sauce.

COLD SAUCES

Dips, dressings and salsas should be seasoned to taste sweet and sour with lemon or lime juice and sugar, honey or some alternative sweetener, such as thick vegetable or fruit juice from a health-food shop. A dash of fresh ginger, coriander powder, fresh chili pepper and caraway will add an exotic

taste. And you can hardly do without onions and garlic.

DESSERT SAUCES

The queen among dessert sauce spices is, of course, vanilla. Cut the black bean lengthways with a knife, scrape out the pulp and warm with the bean in a sauce. This will best bring out the essence. A good vanilla-sugar is also tasty. Dessert sauces can be tastefully seasoned with organic citrus fruit peels. Fruity dessert sauces go best with cinnamon, but also with aniseed, coriander and cardamom powder, allspice, star aniseed and cloves as well as with bay leaf.

WHAT YOU WILL FIND HERE

Although this small lexicon is devoted to sauces, tradional as well as exotic, you will also find dressings, salsas, chutneys, relishes and dips. Apart from the basic recipes for classic meat sauces and marinades, there are piquant sauces to go with meat and poultry, fine sauces for fish, seafood and vegetable courses and, of course, choice sauces for pasta and salads. The last chapter is reserved for heavenly sweet dessert sauces.

The appendix lists everything that you may want to know about sauces: what can be used to thicken a sauce? What to do if you don't like the smell of your sauce? Which sauces are suitable for preserving and freezing? What happens if the sauce curdles? Our emergency guide provides you with all necessary information! We will tell you about it along with explaining some important special terms. And, of course, you will learn what food complements a par-

ticular sauce. With the help of the detailed index, you will quickly find the recipe you're looking for.

There's only one more thing to say: if you enjoy the preparation, your guests will enjoy the taste! Stir and beat, mix and strain and season until your concoction pleases you.

Classic Sauces,
Meat Juices & Marinade

Those who bring a tasty meal to a table always serve a good sauce with it. There are a number of classic sauces whose preparation is not difficult at all if certain rules are observed. Hollandaise sauce is, of course, one. Also Béchamel sauce served over vegetables, horseradish sauce or apple-horseradish which complements boiled meat, mustard sauce which accompanies boiled fish, herb sauce, tomato sauce and, of course, piquant mayonnaise, are all basic sauces.

A strong, reduced broth is fundamental to any sauce. Also, spicy marinades, in which meat and vegetables are preserved, are special aspects of modern cooking.

Hollandaise Sauce

INGREDIENTS: 3 egg yolks • 3 tablespoons white wine • ¾ cups of melted butter • salt • 1 pinch cayenne pepper • juice of ½ lemon

TIP

Maltaise sauce is a variation seasoned with red orange juice and orange zest.

PREPARATION: Whisk the yolks with the white wine over a double boiler until frothy. Add the melted butter carefully with a whisk. Season with salt, cayenne pepper and juice. This warm, whisked sauce can be served not only over fresh, white asparagus or other vegetables, but also with roasted meat.

Lime Hollandaises

INGREDIENTS: 4 egg yolks • 2 teaspoons lime juice • salt • freshly ground white pepper • 9 oz butter • 1 organic lime • freshly ground pepper

PREPARATION: Whisk the yolks with the lime juice. Generously, season with salt and pepper. Cook over a double boiler and whisk constantly until thickened. Continuing to whisk, slowly add warm, melted butter. Wash the lime with hot water, dry and grate 1–2 teaspoons of the peel. Add to the sauce and season with pepper.

Walnut Hollandaise

INGREDIENTS: 4 teaspoons water • 14 husked walnuts • 4 peppercorns, crushed • 1 bay leaf • 3 egg yolks • 6 oz butter • salt • freshly ground pepper • 4 teaspoons raspberry vinegar

PREPARATION: Bring water to a boil. Finely chop 4 walnuts and let boil in water for 2 minutes with the crushed peppercorns and bay leaf. Pour the spiced water through a strainer into a dish. Add yolks and whisk until creamy in a double boiler. Melt the butter over low heat and pour it in a thin stream into the yolk mixture. Keep stirring until the sauce is creamy. Chop the remaining walnuts and add to the sauce. Season to taste with salt, pepper and raspberry vinegar.

TIP
This sauce is especially delectable with a fresh vegetable plate of asparagus, young carrots, sugar husks, spring onions, celery stalks, broccoli and poached eggs.

Red Hollandaise with Thyme

INGREDIENTS: 5 oz butter • 3 teaspoons tomato paste • 1 teaspoon fresh thyme leaves • 3 egg yolks • 4 teaspoons red wine • cayenne pepper • sugar

PREPARATION: Melt the butter over low heat and stir in the tomato paste at room temperature with a whisk. Add thyme leaves. Whisk the yolks and red wine in a double boiler until creamy. Add the tomato paste slowly in a thin stream and continue to stir. Season to taste with salt, Cayenne pepper and sugar.

Lobster-Hollandaise

TIP
Lobster-Hollandaise goes well with grilled or steamed fish and seafood.

INGREDIENTS: 2 cups lobster meat juice • 1 teaspoon ground • 1 bay leaf • 1 piece of lime peel • 3 egg yolks • 6 oz butter • salt • freshly ground pepper • 1 teaspoons chopped dill • 3 – 4 teaspoons lime juice

PREPARATION: Thicken the lobster meat juice with the spices over high heat and then pour through a strainer into a dish. Add the yolks and whisk the mixture in a double boiler until creamy.

Mousseline Sauce

INGREDIENTS: 1 portion Hollandaise Sauce (see page 16) • 3½ oz cream • dash of sweet pepper powder

PREPARATION: Whip the cream until thick with a little pepper powder and add it to the lukewarm Hollandaise Sauce. Serve immediately.

TIP
This fine sauce tastes especially good with white and green asparagus and cauliflower.

Béchamel Sauce

INGREDIENTS: 3 tablespoons butter • 2 ½ tablespoons flour • 1 quart milk • 1 bay leaf • 5 peppercorns • 2 thyme stalks • salt • freshly ground pepper • freshly grated nutmeg • 1 egg yolk, if desired.

PREPARATION: Melt the butter, add the flour and cook lightly. Gradually add the milk to the roux and stir until smooth. Add the bay leaf, crushed peppercorn and thyme stalks and let simmer in a covered pot over low heat for 10 minutes. Strain the sauce through a strainer and season with salt, pepper and nutmeg. Finally, add the yolks to the moderately hot (not boiling!) sauce.

TIP
To make the Béchamelsauce especially spicy, cook 2 oz bacon and 1 chopped onion in the butter. Add flour, milk and spices, cook then strain.

Creamy Chive Sauce

TIP
This sauce can also be prepared with dill, chervil, parsley or a mixture of various herbs.

INGREDIENTS: 2 teaspoons mustard seeds • 2 cups of cream • 4 oz of cold butter • salt • freshly ground white pepper • 2 tablespoons lemon juice • 1–2 bunches chives

PREPARATION: Crush half of the mustard seeds and let them boil in 5 tablespoons of water for about 5 minutes. Strain. Add the rest of the mustard seeds and boil with 1 ¾ cup cream for about 15 minutes. Add the cold butter to the sauce in pieces. Season with

salt, pepper and lemon juice. Chop the chives and add to the sauce. Whip the rest of the cream until it is halfway thick, then stir into the sauce.

Tarragon Sauce

INGREDIENTS: 2 eggs • juice of 1 lemon • 1 ¾ cups of cream • 4 teaspoons mustard, medium hot • 4 tablespoons tarragon vinegar • 2 bunches tarragon • olive oil • salt • freshly ground pepper

PREPARATION: Mix the eggs, lemon juice, cream, mustard and tarragon vinegar. Add finely chopped tarragon and season to taste with olive oil, salt and pepper. This sauce can be varied to please the eye and tongue if 2–3 peeled and cubed tomatos are added to the sauce before preparation.

> **TIP**
> Freshly whisked, foamy sauces should be served immediately as they lose their consistency quickly.

Sabayon with Basil

INGREDIENTS: 1 garlic clove • 3 egg yolks • 1 cup dry white wine • 1 tablespoon lemon juice • ½ teaspoon starch • 1 tablespoon white port wine • 1 tablespoon tomato purée • salt • freshly ground white pepper • 4 tablespoons chopped basil

PREPARATION: Rub the inside of a bowl with the peeled garlic. Add the yolks, white wine, lemon juice and starch and stir until smooth. Mix the port wine with the tomato purée and add to the wine mixture. Cook in a double boiler until creamy. Season to taste with salt and pepper and, finally, stir in the basil.

Herb Sauce

INGREDIENTS: 1 teaspoon mustard • ½ cup yogurt • 1 tablespoon lemon juice • salt • freshly ground pepper • 2 tablespoons chopped herbs (parsley, chives, chervil, dill, coriander) • 7 tablespoons cream

PREPARATION: Stir the mustard, yogurt and lemon juice until smooth, season with salt and pepper and add the herbs. Whip the cream thick and add to the herb sauce. The herbs can, of course, be varied according to your taste or to what you have growing in your herb garden.

Yogurt Herb Sauce

INGREDIENTS: 6 tablespoons fresh herbs • 2 small shallots • 2 cloves of garlic • 3 cups cream yogurt • 2 tablespoons olive oil • 2 tablespoons balm vinegar • salt • freshly ground pepper

PREPARATION: Wash the herbs, dry them and chop finely. Peel the shallots and mince. Peel and press the garlic. Mix it, together with the other ingredients, into a smooth sauce and season with salt and pepper. If desired, you can leave out the garlic from this wonderfully fresh sauce.

Tomato Basil Sauce

INGREDIENTS: 6 tomatos • 2 bundles basil • 3 shallots • 3 teaspoons butter • 6 teaspoons sherry or white wine vinegar • ¼ cup cooking oil • 2 cups white wine • 3 tablespoons lemon juice • salt • freshly ground pepper

PREPARATION: Wash the tomatos, halve them and dice. Wash and dry the basil and cut into fine strips. Peel the shallots, mince and sauté briefly in butter. Then add vinegar, oil, white wine and lemon juice. Boil the liquid until reduced by a third. Add the tomatos and basil and season with salt and pepper. Tomato Basil Sauce can be served warm or cold with asparagus.

Creamy Horseradish Sauce

> **TIP**
> Creamy Horseradish Sauce is marvelous with boiled beef or ox with potatoes, but it is also tasty with carp and other boiled freshwater fish.

INGREDIENTS: 1 cup cream • 1 piece horseradish, peeled and finely grated • salt • sugar • 1 teaspoon lemon juice

PREPARATION: Whip the cold cream until thick. Add the horseradish to the cream. Season with salt, sugar and lemon juice.

Apple Horseradish sauce

> **TIP**
> Freshly grated horseradish is very tasty, but you can also use grated horseradish from a jar. If you don't like it so hot, add less to the sauce.

INGREDIENTS: 2 slightly sour apples • 1 teaspoon honey • 4 tablespoons horseradish • a little Worcestershire sauce • salt

PREPARATION: Quarter, peel and core the apples. Cut into small cubes and boil in a little water. Stir the boiled apples vigorously with a whisk, then set aside to cool. Add the honey and horseradish and season with Worcestershire sauce and salt.

Barbecue Sauce

INGREDIENTS: 5 tablespoons hot mustard (Dijon mustard is the best) • 5 tablespoons dry white wine • 5 tablespoons mild honey (e.g. honey from lime-tree flower) • 3 tablespoons soy sauce • 2 tablespoons sunflower oil • 5 tablespoons tomato ketchup • salt • freshly ground black pepper • tabasco or chili-oil.

PREPARATION: Combine the mustard, wine, honey, soy sauce, oil and ketchup in a pot and simmer over medium heat for about 5 minutes. Season with salt, pepper and tabasco or chili-oil and leave to cool.

TIP
Barbecue sauce is good with steaks, spare ribs chicken wings and grilled meat. If desired, you can mix a little fresh garlic into the prepared sauce.

English Mint Sauce

INGREDIENTS: 5 tablespoons finely chopped fresh mint • 5 tablespoons good white wine vinegar • 2 teaspoons sugar

PREPARATION: Put the mint leaves in a small dish and pour a little hot water over them. Let cool. Add the vinegar and sugar. Cover for several hours before serving.

TIP
Mint sauce is a favourite, especially in Great Britain, and is usually served with lamb.

Sabayon

TIP

If you choose to leave out alcohol, include a corresponding amount of vegetable or chicken broth in this foamy sauce.

INGREDIENTS: 4 egg yolks • 1 cup dry white wine • 1 teaspoon lemon juice • 1 tablespoon dry vermouth • ½ teaspoon starch • salt • freshly ground white pepper • 1 tablespoon chopped tarragon • 1 tablespoon chopped parsley

PREPARATION: Whisk the yolks with the vermouth until smooth, then add lemon juice and starch. Gradually add the white wine, stirring constantly. Whisk and cook in a double boiler intil creamy. Season the sauce with salt and pepper. Finally, add the herbs.

Cheesey Cream Sauce

INGREDIENTS: 2 cups cream • 18 oz young Gouda cheese • salt • freshly ground white pepper • 1 bunch basil • 4 tomatos or 2 ripe peaches

TIP

This quick and easy sauce is best with pasta, but is also good with vegetables.

PREPARATION: Bring the cream to a boil. Finely grate the cheese. Add the cheese bit by bit into the hot (not boiling!) cream. Stir until the sauce is creamy. Season with salt and pepper. Pluck basil leaves from their stems and chop them finely. Mix with the sauce. Peel tomatoes or peaches, core and cut them into small pieces and stir them into the sauce.

Cheese Sauce

INGREDIENTS: 1 package of light sauce for 1 cup of milk • 7 oz processed cream cheese • 5 oz Crème Fraîche • salt • freshly ground pepper • 1 tablespoon lemon juice • grated peel of organic lemon • 5 tablespoons grated parmesan • a little chopped parsley

TIP
This sauce gets lighter and goes well especially with asparagus if, instead of milk, the boiled asparagus water is used in the preparation.

PREPARATION: Mix the sauce powder in the liquid and bring to a boil. Add the processed cheese and stir. Add the Crème Fraîche and season with the salt, pepper and lemon juice. Mix the lemon peel with the parmesan and parsley and sprinkle over the sauce before serving.

Olive Egg Sauce

INGREDIENTS: 2 hard boiled eggs • 2 tablespoons (pitted) black olives • 1 tablespoon fresh herbs, 1 teaspoons capers • 1 anchovy fillet • 6 tablespoons olive oil • 3 tablespoons white wine vinegar • freshly ground pepper • salt

PREPARATION: Shell the eggs, separate the whites from the yolks and chop finely. Chop the olives, herbs, capers and anchovy fillet finely, stir in the oil and vinegar and add the egg whites and yolks. Season with pepper and salt.

Fruit Sauce with Mustard

TIP
This fruity sauce tastes good both cold and warm. It is suitable with grilled meat, poultry and for meat fondue.

INGREDIENTS: 1 organic orange • 1 apple • 1 tablespoon butter • salt • freshly ground pepper • 1 teaspoon honey • 5 tablespoons stewed cranberries • 1 tablespoon Dijon-mustard • 2 tablespoons grated horseradish • 1 tablespoon lemon juice

PREPARATION: Wash the orange in hot water, dry it and grate the skin. Peel the apple and the orange and cut into fine cubes. Saute in hot butter until soft. Add the salt, pepper, honey, stewed cranberries, mustard, horse radish, orange peel and lemon juice.

Tuna Sauce

INGREDIENTS: 2 shallots • 1 tablespoon olive oil • 6 anchovies • 1 ½ tablespoons capers • salt • sugar • freshly ground white pepper • 2 cans tuna in oil • 4 tablespoons mayonnaise • 3 ½ tablespoons cream • 3 tablespoons dry wine • 1 lemon • 1 tablespoon chopped parsley

PREPARATION: Peel the shallots, chop them finely and saute until glassy in olive oil. Add anchovies and capers, and season with salt, sugar and pepper and set aside to cool. Strain the tuna, add spices, mayonnaise, cream, white wine, cooled onion and purée finely in a food processor or blender. Season the sauce again with salt, sugar and pepper. Garnish with parsley.

TIP
This sauce is suitable for making Vitello tonnato, veal in tuna sauce. Cut the boiled meat into thin slices, cover them with the sauce and set aside for 24 hours. Garnish with slices of lemon, parsley and black olives.

Walnut Honey Sauce

INGREDIENTS: 3 oz mixed pickles chopped into small cubes • 6 tablespoons chopped walnuts • 6 tablespoons chopped almonds • 2 tablespoons honey • 2 tablespoons white bread crumbs • 3 tablespoons mustard seed juice • salt • freshly ground black pepper

PREPARATION: Combine the fruit, nuts, honey and bread crumbs. Add the mustard seed juice and season with salt and pepper.

TIP
This attractive, hot and sweet combination complements smoked pork and boiled ham.

Spinach Sauce

TIP
This is a sauce rich in vitamins, especially suitable with new potatoes, poached eggs, and omelettes.

INGREDIENTS: 7 oz frozen creamed spinach • 2 onions • 2 tablespoons butter • 1 cup Crème Fraîche • salt • freshly ground pepper • freshly ground nutmeg

PREPARATION: Thaw the spinach and peel the onions. Melt the butter and saute the onions until transparent. Add the spinach and heat. Add the Crème Fraîche and season with salt, pepper and nutmeg.

Avocado Sauce

INGREDIENTS: 1 package of Sauce Hollandaise (1 cup) • 2 avocados • juice of 1 lemon • 1 pinch sugar • freshly ground pepper

PREPARATION: Boil the Sauce Hollandaise. Halve the avocados, remove the pits, remove the pulp from the shell with a spoon, purée it and mix with lemon juice. Add the avocado purée to the Hollandaise sauce and season with sugar and pepper.

> **TIP**
> You shouldn't leave this creamy sauce standing for a long time because it loses its appetizing green color fast.

Almond Garlic Sauce

INGREDIENTS: 1 head of garlic • 4 slices white bread without crust • 1 organic lemon • 5 tablespoons ground almonds • 5 tablespoons olive oil • coarse salt • pepper

PREPARATION: Divide the garlic into cloves, peel, chop coarsely and crush together with salt in a mortar. Grate the lemon peel and dice the bread. Add the bread, almonds and lemon juice to the garlic in the mortar and make a paste. Season with pepper and a little lemon zest. Add oil in drops until the sauce thickens.

White Wine Sauce

TIP
This quick sauce tastes great when make with tarragon or romanesque mustard.

INGREDIENTS: 3 tablespoons dry white wine • 2 tablespoons spicy mustard • 6 tablespoons mayonnaise • salt • cayenne pepper

PREPARATION: Stir wine, mustard and mayonnaise till smooth, then season with salt and cayenne.

Garlic Sauce

INGREDIENTS: 3 ½ oz white bread • ½ cup vegetable broth • 1 egg yolk • salt • freshly ground black pepper • 2–4 garlic cloves • ½ cup olive oil • 1 tablespoon chopped parsley

TIP
Garlic sauce is suitable for all grilled meals, whether meat, fish or vegetables. It is also delicious spread on bread.

PREPARATION: Chop the white bread, remove the crust and soak in the vegetable broth. Purée with the yolk, salt and pepper in a mixer. Peel the garlic cloves, chop them coarsely and add gradually with the olive oil into the mixer. Purée till smooth. Pour into a dish and sprinkle with parsley before serving.

Béarnaise Sauce

INGREDIENTS: 7 tablespoons white wine • 3 tablespoons tarragon vinegar • 1 shallot cut, minced • 1 teaspoon fresh tarragon, coarsely chopped • 3 peppercorns, coarsely crushed • 4 egg yolks • ¾ cup melted butter • salt • cayenne pepper • 1 teaspoon finely chopped tarragon • 1 teaspoon finely chopped parsley

> **TIP**
> Choron sauce is a variation, seasoned with tomato paste and chopped herbs.

PREPARATION: Heat the white wine with the vinegar, shallot, tarragon and pepper and let simmer for 2 minutes. Strain and set aside to cool. Whisk the yolks with white wine in a double boiler until frothy. Remove the sauce from the heat and gradually whisk in the melted butter. Season with salt, cayenne pepper and fresh herbs.

Bacon Herb Sauce

INGREDIENTS: 4 spring onions • 2 tablespoons butter •
4 oz bacon • 1 pickled cucumber • 1 green chili pepper •
1 cup mixed, chopped herbs • ¾ cup Crème Fraîche • sugar • 4 tablespoons whipped cream

PREPARATION: Clean and cut the spring onions
into small pieces. Saute in the butter until soft.
Chop the bacon and fry until crisp. Grate the
cucumber finely and mince the chili pepper.
Mix all the small, finely cut ingredients with the
herbs and the Crème Fraîche and heat everything. Season with salt and sugar. Finally, stir
the cream into the mixture.

Bacon Gravy

INGREDIENTS: 14 oz bacon • 1 teaspoon dried marjoram •
2 tomatoes • ½ cup meat broth • 2 tablespoons chopped
chives

TIP
This rustic sauce tastes
best with mashed pota-
toes.

PREPARATION: Chop the bacon and fry over medium
heat. Stir in the marjoram. Peel, core and dice the
tomatoes. Add to bacon along with the broth and
chives and serve hot.

Mustard Egg Sauce

INGREDIENTS: 4 tablespoons melted butter • 6 tablespoons olive oil • 8 tablespoons vegetable broth • 2 tablespoons Dijon-mustard • 1 tablespoon sweet mustard • 4 table-spoons mixed pickles • 2 hard boiled eggs • salt • freshly ground pepper • 2 tablespoons chopped dill

PREPARATION: Stir the butter with the oil, broth and mustards until smooth. Chop the pickles very finely. Shell the eggs and chop them finely as well. Stir pickles and eggs into the sauce. Season with salt, pepper and dill. Serve the sauce at room temperature.

Pepper Yogurt Sauce

INGREDIENTS: 1 red pepper pod • 1 cup vegetable broth • 7 tablespoons cream • 3 teaspoon starch • 1 tablespoon paprika • ¾ cup cream yogurt • salt • honey • cayenne pepper

PREPARATION: Peel the chilli pepper with a special peeler and clean it. Cut about a quarter of the pepper very finely into cubes. Boil the rest in the broth until soft. Purée it. Mix the cream with starch and paprika and pour into the hot broth. Let boil once. Add the raw pepper cubes with the jogurt, but do not let it boil. Season the sauce with salt, honey and cayenne pepper.

Mushroom Sauce

TIP
Pink mushrooms, known as Egerlinge, are richer in taste than white ones.

INGREDIENTS: 1 onion • 1 clove of garlic • 5 oz mushrooms • 4 tablespoons butter • 1 tablespoon flour • 1 cup meat broth • 2 tablespoons cream • salt • freshly ground white pepper • freshly ground nutmeg • a little lemon juice • 2 tablespoons chopped parsley

PREPARATION: Peel and chop onions and garlic finely. Clean and cut mushrooms into small pieces. Sauté onion, garlic and mushrooms in 2 tablespoons of hot butter for 5 minutes and purée with a mixer. Melt the rest of the butter, stir in flour and cook for a short time. Pour the meat broth in gradually and let simmer slowly in a covered pot for 10 minutes. Stir in mushrooms and cream and season with pungent spices.

Chantilly Sauce

TIP
This creamy sauce is suitable for seafood and light, grilled meat as well as for meat fondue.

INGREDIENTS: 2 tablespoons mayonnaise • 1 teaspoon tomato paste • 1 tablespoon dry sherry • 1 teaspoon lemon juice • 1 teaspoon Dijon-mustard • salt • chili powder • sugar • 3 ½ oz whipped cream

PREPARATION: Mix mayonnaise with tomato paste, sherry, lemon juice and mustard. Season to taste with salt, chili powder and sugar. Finally, stir in cream.

Orange Sauce

INGREDIENTS: 3 organic oranges • 1 organic lemon • 1 red onion • 1 bunch rosemary • 7 tablespoons semi-dry white wine • 1 teaspoon starch • 1 tablespoon ginger jam

PREPARATION: Peel off strips of skin from 1 orange and 1 lemon with a peeling tool. Press out all the fruit. Cut onions very finely into cubes. Boil citrus juice with rosemary, white wine and the fine citrus strips for 5 minutes. Stir starch with a little water until smooth, pour it into the juice and let boil once. Stir in ginger jam.

Lemon Sauce

INGREDIENTS: 1 onion • 1 clove of garlic • 2 tablespoons butter • 1 cup chicken broth • 3 teaspoons of light sauce starch • 9 oz mascarpone • 1 organic lemon • salt • chili pepper powder • sugar

> **TIP**
> Citrus juices go well with roast poultry or veal liver and rice.

PREPARATION: Peel and cut onion and garlic into small pieces and cook them in butter. Pour broth over all and sprinkle sauce starch on the surface. Let it boil for a short time. Stir mascarpone into the hot, no longer boiling sauce. Add lemon juice and peel to the sauce and season with salt, chili pepper powder and sugar.

Tomato Sugo

INGREDIENTS: 1 bunch soup herbs • 2 sticks celery • 2 onions • 3 cloves of garlic • 4 tablespoons olive oil • 3 tablespoons tomato paste • 1 big can of peeled tomatoes • 2 bay leaves • 2 sprigs thyme • 1 sprig rosemary • 1 red chili pepper • salt • freshly ground pepper • sugar • 4 tomatoes

PREPARATION: Clean the herbs and celery, peel the onions and garlic, cut everything into small pieces. Heat oil and cook ingredients in it for a short time. Stir in the tomato paste and simmer for a short time. Add tomatoes and bay leaves and let simmer uncovered for 15 minutes. Stir in sprigs of herbs and chili pepper chopped into small pieces and let simmer for another 15 minutes. Season with salt, pepper and sugar. Peel, core and cut the tomatoes into small pieces. Stir into sugo and remove the springs of spice.

Tomato Sauce

INGREDIENTS: 1 clove garlic • 2 tablespoons olive oil • 1 tablespoon butter • 26 oz tomatoes • 2 tablespoons tomato paste • 2 tablespoons tomato ketchup • 1 teaspoon dried oregano • salt • freshly ground pepper • sugar

PREPARATION: Peel and chop garlic finely. Heat oil and butter, stir in garlic. Wash tomatoes, quarter them and cut off the stems. Add along with tomato paste and ketchup to garlic and simmer for 10 minutes. Then strain. Spice with oregano, salt, pepper and sugar and let it simmer uncovered 5 minutes more.

Bolognese Meat Sauce

INGREDIENTS: 1 bunch soup herbs • 2 cloves of garlic • 3 ½ oz Parmesan • 6 tablespoons olive oil • 18 oz mixed ground meat • ½ cup red wine • 1 bay leaf • 2 cloves • 1 stick thyme • 2 cans pizza tomatoes • 2 tablespoons tomato paste • salt • freshly ground pepper • sugar • 4 tablespoons chopped parsley

PREPARATION: Clean the soup herbs, peel and cut garlic and herbs, together with ham, into small pieces. Heat 4 tablespoons olive oil and cook for a short time.

Add the ground meat and roast until crumbly. Add red wine and stir in bay leaf, cloves, thyme, tomatoes and tomato paste. Let the sauce simmer uncovered for 30 minutes. Remove all solid spices, season with salt, pepper and sugar and let simmer uncovered 10 minutes more. Mix in parsley and remaining oil.

TIP
There are numerous variations of this favourite Italian pasta sauce, Ragú di carne: without tomatoes, with capers, with ground veal, with cream.

Pesto

> **TIP**
> Always make this pasta sauce with fresh ingredients. It does not keep well and quickly loses its appetizing looks and fresh taste. If you like a thinner sauce, mix about 1 cup boiling water with pesto and serve with pasta.

INGREDIENTS: 2–3 cloves of garlic • 4 tablespoons pine nuts • 60 fresh basil leaves • 5 tablespoons grated Parmesan or Pecorino • 8 ½ tablespoons – 1 ¾ cups olive oil • salt

PREPARATION: Peel and cut garlic into small pieces. Chop the pine nuts coarsely. Cut basil leaves coarsely with the kitchen scissors. Mash all the ingredients into a paste with a mortar. Add cheese and pour in oil in a thin stream, process it all to a smooth, creamy sauce. The process is facilitated with a mixer. If desired, season with salt.

Bagnet Rosso

INGREDIENTS: 1 shallot • 2 cloves garlic • 1 boiled carrot • ½ peeled yellow pepper • 2 peeled and seeded tomatoes • 1 pickled cucumber • 1 red chili pepper • 1 tablespoon small capers • 1 tablespoon anchovy paste • 1 teaspoon coarse mustard • 1–2 tablespoons breadcrumbs • ½ cup olive oil • white wine vinegar • salt • freshly ground pepper • sugar • 2 tablespoons chopped parsley.

PREPARATION: Peel and cut shallot and garlic with carrot, pepper, tomato, pickled cucumber and chili pepper into very small cubes. Mix with capers. Mix anchovy paste with mustard, some breadcrumbs and oil. Mix with vegetables and season with vinegar, salt, pepper and sugar. If desired, add some more breadcrumbs and stir in parsley.

Cumberland Sauce

INGREDIENTS: 1 shallot • ½ cup strong red wine • ½ cup port wine • 1 bay leaf • 10 peppercorns • 1 organic orange • 4 tablespoons red currant jelly • a little Worcesteshire sauce • 3–4 tablespoons red wine vinegar

PREPARATION: Peel shallot and cut finely. Bring to boil together with red wine and port wine. Add bay leaf and crushed grains of pepper and boil down to half. Wash and dry the orange. Peel its skin in strips and press out fruit. Pour the reduced wine and the orange juice through a strainer. Add red currant jelly, about 1 teaspoon Worcestershire sauce, vinegar and orange strips and let mixture boil uncovered at medium heat for 15–20 minutes.

TIP
This cold, sharply sweet sauce is great for meat and venison patés as well as for venison roasted for a short time, veal, poultry and, of course, meat fondue.

Devil Sauce

INGREDIENTS: 5 tablespoons Pancetta • 4 tablespoons olive oil • 1 bunch spring onions • 3 cloves garlic • 26 oz tomatoes • 1 red pepper • 2 red chili pepper pods • a little tomato paste • 2 tablespoons soy sauce • 1 tablespoon balsamic vinegar • 1 teaspoon honey • salt • freshly ground pepper • 5 big basil leaves

PREPARATION: Cut Pancetta into fine cubes and cook for a short time in hot oil. Clean spring onions, peel garlic, chop both and cook for a short time with bacon. Peel and core tomatoes and cut coarsely into cubes. Add to the onions and cook for a few minutes.
Meanwhile, peel and cut pepper finely into cubes. Cook chili pepper with or without pips. Stir pepper, chili, a little tomato juice and soy sauce into onion-tomato mixture and bring to boil once more. Season with balsamic vinegar, honey, salt and pepper. Cut the basil leaves into strips and sprinkle them over the cooled sauce.

Asparagus Sauce

INGREDIENTS: 18 oz asparagus • salt • sugar • ½ cup white wine • 1 organic lemon • 3 egg yolks • 2 tablespoons soy sauce • 1 knife tip grated ginger • 1 cup melted butter • salt • freshly ground white pepper

PREPARATION: Peel and cut asparagus into small pieces. Mix a little salt and sugar with wine and boil asparagus in the mixture until it is very soft. Separate 3 tablespoons of the boiling water. Drain and purée asparagus with some of the broth. Wash the lemon in hot water and dry it. Peel off a little of the lemon's skin and press out the fruit. Whisk yolks until creamy with the reserved broth in a double boiler. Stir in soy sauce and ginger. Pour in butter in a thin stream and continue stirring. Finally, add the puréed asparagus and a little more broth. Season with salt, lemon juice and lemon peel.

Red Wine Sauce

INGREDIENTS: 3 ½ oz ground beef • 2 tablespoons oil • 1 onion • 1 garlic clove • 1 bunch of soup herbs • 1 tablespoon tomato paste • 2 cups red wine • 1 bay leaf • 1 clove • salt • freshly ground pepper • 2 tablespoons soy sauce • 5 tablespoons chilled butter

PREPARATION: Cook ground beef in hot oil. Peel onion and garlic, clean the soup herbs and cut everything into small pieces. Cook onion, garlic, the soup herbs and tomato paste with meat once more. Add red wine, bay leaf and clove, let it all simmer for 15–20 minutes and then pour it through a strainer. Season the sauce with salt, pepper and soy sauce. Stir cold butter into it in pieces. As soon as the sauce is well-blended, take it off the boil.

Mustard Sauce with Meat Rissoles

INGREDIENTS: ½ cup meat broth • ½ cup cream • 3 teaspoons Mondamin Roast Meat Juice • 3 tablespoons light classic roux • 2 tablespoons coarse mustard • salt • freshly ground pepper

PREPARATION: Loosen roast grounds with broth and cream. Stir in the meat juice and let it boil once. Add roux to the sauce and season it with mustard, salt and pepper.

Hunter's Sauce with Escalope

INGREDIENTS: 2 tablespoons butter • 1 onion • 7 oz mushrooms • 1 cup meat broth • 3 tablespoons white wine • 2 teaspoons Mondamin Roast Meat Juice • 2 tomatoes • 3–4 tablespoons dark starch sauce • salt • freshly ground pepper • 2 tablespoons chopped parsley

PREPARATION: Cook roast grounds with butter. Peel and cut onion into cubes. Clean mushrooms and cut heads into thin slices.

Add onion and mushrooms to butter and cook briefly. Add broth and wine, stir in the meat juice and boil. Peel, core and cut tomatoes into cubes. Add to sauce and bind with sauce starch, salt, pepper and parsley.

Pepper Sauce with Steaks

INGREDIENTS: 1 cup bouillon • 2 tablespoons pickled green peppercorns • 3 teaspoons Mondamin Bratenfond thickening preparation • 3 tablespoons dark sauce binder • salt • fresh ground pepper • 2 tablespoons whipped cream

PREPARATION: Loosen roast meat grounds with bouillon. Crush peppercorns gently and add to bouillon. Stir in the Bratenfond and brings to boil once. Bind the sauce with sauce binder and spice with salt and pepper. Fold in whipped cream at the end.

Onion Sauce with Cutlets

INGREDIENTS: 2 tablespoons butter • 1 teaspoon sugar • 1 cup onions • ½ cup bouillon • ½ cup red wine • 3 teaspoons Mondamin Bratenfond • 3 tablespoons classic dark roux • salt • fresh ground pepper

PREPARATION: Melt butter in juice of roasted meat, and melt sugar in it. Peel onion and cut in fine semi-circles. Add onion to the butter and roast until golden. Add bouillon, red wine and Bratenfond to the onion and bring to boil once more. Bind the sauce with roux and spice with salt and pepper.

Creamy Mustard Sauce

INGREDIENTS: 8 tablespoons olive oil • 8 tablespoons cream • 8 tablespoons drawn butter • 10 tablespoons fish bouillon • 4 tablespoons Dijon mustard • 1 tablespoon sweetish mustard • 1 tablespoon granulated mustard • salt • sugar • 1 tablespoon cut dill

TIP
This fast but tasty mustard sauce goes well with boiled fish, seafood and poached eggs.

PREPARATION: Heat oil, cream, butter and bouillon and mix well. Add all mustards and spice with salt, sugar and dill.

Frankfurt Green Sauce

INGREDIENTS: 9 oz mixed herbs (parsley, watercress, dock, pimpinella, chives, beaked parsley) • 2 hard-boiled eggs • 1 pickle • 1 cup yogurt • 1 cup sour cream • 1 teaspoon Dijon mustard • dash lemon juice • salt • fresh ground pepper

TIP
A supplement to potatoes, boiled fish and boiled beef, rich in vitamins.

PREPARATION: Clean, wash and cut the herbs fine. Peel eggs and cut in little cubes as well as the pickle. Mix yogurt, cream, mustard and little lemon juice. Add the herbs, cubed eggs and pickle. Flavor with salt and pepper.

Italian Vinaigrette

INGREDIENTS: 2 tablespoons raisins • 2 tablespoons Grappa • 2 tablespoons pine nuts • 3 tablespoons balsamic vinegar • 1 tablespoon lemon juice • 8 tablespoons olive oil • 1 tablespoon little capers • 1 small, cut, red chili pepper • salt • fresh ground pepper

PREPARATION: Soak the raisins in Grappa for several hours. Roast pine nuts. Mix vinegar with lemon juice and oil until creamy. Add raisins, pine nuts, capers and chili. Spice with salt and pepper.

Orange Vinaigrette

INGREDIENTS: Juice and peel of 1 chemically untreated orange • 6 tablespoons olive oil • 3 tablespoons lemon juice • 1 teaspoon honey made from orange blossoms • salt • crushed red peppercorns • 1 teaspoon fresh thyme leaves

PREPARATION: Mix the orange juice with orange peel, oil, mustard and honey until creamy. Spice with salt and add crushed peppercorns and thyme leaves.

Mayonnaise

INGREDIENTS: 2 yolks • 1 teaspoon sharp mustard • 1 tablespoon lemon juice • 1 cup sunflower oil • salt • fresh ground white pepper • sugar

PREPARATION: Mix yolks in a dish with mustard and lemon juice well. Add oil in drops stirring constantly. When the sauce is slightly creamy, pour in a thin stream of oil. Spice the mayonnaise with salt, pepper and sugar so that it is piquant.

Remoulade Sauce

INGREDIENTS: Mayonnaise (see above) • 2 tablespoons cubed spicy pickles • 1 tablespoon cut capers • 1 tablespoon cut beaked parsley or estragon • a little pickle juice

PREPARATION: Mix mayonnaise and all the other ingredients and thin with pickle juice.

Tatar Sauce

INGREDIENTS: Mayonnaise (see above) • 1 hard-boiled egg yolk • 2 cut shallots • 2 tablespoons cut capers • 1 tablespoon Dijon mustard • 1 tablespoon cut parsley

PREPARATION: Mix mayonnaise with yolk passed through a sieve, shallots, capers, mustard and parsley.

Aioli

INGREDIENTS: 1 hard-boiled egg yolk • 4–6 garlic cloves, minced • mayonnaise (page 48)

PREPARATION: Purée yolk with some hot water and garlic cloves and mix with mayonnaise.

Rouille

INGREDIENTS: 1 cleaned red pepper • 6 tablespoons cut pickled peppers • 2 red cut chili peppers • 4 peeled and cut garlic cloves • 6 tablespoons olive oil • 2–4 tablespoons fresh grated white bread • salt

PREPARATION: Cook raw pepper in little water until tender. In a mortar or mixer mash with the pickled pepper, chili, garlic and oil. To get a creamy sauce, mix in white bread as desired and spice with salt.

Tapenade

INGREDIENTS: 7 oz black pitted olives • 2 oz green pitted olives • 2 oz anchovy fillets • 3 tablespoons cut capers • a little lemon peel and lemon juice • 6–8 tablespoons olive oil

PREPARATION: Mash all ingredients in a mortar or in a mixer.

TIP
Tapenade is popular in southern France where one spreads it onto a toasted baguette and serves it with aperitif.

Anchoiade

INGREDIENTS: 3½ oz finely cubed shallots • 1 peeled garlic clove • 1 teaspoon butter • 7 oz anchovy fillets • 4 tablespoons olive oil • 3–4 tablespoons lemon juice • a little lemon peel • 4 tablespoons chopped Italian parsley.

PREPARATION: Sauté shallots and garlic briefly in hot butter. Dry anchovy fillets and blend with the remaining ingredients in a mixer. Mix with parsley.

Poultry Stock

INGREDIENTS: 3 lbs poultry (chicken, chicken wings) • 4 tablespoons sunflower oil • 1 bunch soup greens • 2 stalks thyme • 2 bay leaves • 1 peeled onion with 3 cloves in it • peel of 1 chemically untreated lemon • 1 teaspoon peppercorns • 1 cup white wine • salt

PREPARATION: Wash the chicken and slightly roast in hot oil until brown. Add 1 quart of water and bring to a simmer. Remove froth from the surface often. Clean greens. Cut in big cubes. After 45 minutes, add to stock, along with herbs, onion and wine and simmer uncovered for 30 minutes more. Pass the bouillon through a sieve and boil down to half to get strong stock.

TIP

Stock is strong boiled-down bouillon. To prepare bouillon, the basis of a soup or a stew, the liquid is simmered only little in order to intensify its taste.

Vegetable Stock

TIP

Stock will have a very nice color if a little turmeric, saffron or onion peel is added to the broth. Or halve an onion brown the cut surface in a dry pan and add to bouillon.

INGREDIENTS: 3 lbs vegetables (carrot, celery, leek, mushrooms, tomatoes, pepper, cabbage, asparagus, kohlrabi, fennel) • 3 bay leaves • 1 peeled onion with 3 cloves in it • 2 stalks thyme • 1 stalk rosemary • 1 pinch saffron powder • 1 teaspoon peppercorns • 1 peeled garlic clove • salt

PREPARATION: Clean the vegetables. Peel and cut in big cubes. Simmer them uncovered in 1 quart of water with all the remaining ingredients for 60 minutes. Pass the liquid through a sieve and boil down to half.

Beef or Veal Stock

INGREDIENTS: 2 lbs beef or veal bones cut in small pieces • 4 tablespoons sunflower oil • 2 tablespoons tomato purée • 2 big onions • 2 carrots • 2 leek stalks • 2 stalks celery • 1 parsley root • ½ celery root • 2 garlic cloves • 4 tomatoes • 3½ oz mushrooms • 3 bay leaves • 1 teaspoon peppercorns • 3 cloves • 2 stalks of thyme • 1 stalk rosemary • 1 bottle of red wine • salt.

PREPARATION: Wash the bones thoroughly and brown well in hot oil. Mix in tomato purée, roast for a while and add 1 quart of water. Simmer in a closed pot for about 90 minutes. Remove froth from the surface often. Clean the vegetables, peel and cut in big cubes. Add the vegetables as well as all spices and herbs and wine to the bones and simmer uncovered for 1 more hour. Pass the stock through a sieve and boil down to half.

> **TIP**
> In order to prepare game bouillon or stock, one needs game bones, very strong red wine, 7 oz mushrooms and enough thyme and rosemary.

Fish Stock

INGREDIENTS: 2 lb white fish bones • 1 peeled onion with 2 cloves in it • ½ fennel root • 2 stalks celery • 1 carrot • 1 stalk leek • 1 peeled garlic clove • 1 cup white wine • 2 bay leaves • 1 teaspoon fennel seeds • 1 teaspoon peppercorns • 1 teaspoon pimento corns • 1 teaspoon mustard seeds • salt

PREPARATION: Wash the fish bones well and bring to boil with 1 quart of water and onion. Remove froth from the surface often. Clean the vegetables and cut in big cubes. Add to fish stock along with white wine and all spices and simmer uncovered for 30 minutes. Pass the liquid through a sieve and boil down until the stock is strong and salty.

> **TIP**
> Do not cook fish bones for more than 30 minutes, otherwise, the liquid will be murky.

Buttermilk Marinade for Game

TIP

Marinating - pickling in a marinade - should make the meat more tender; however it becomes drier as well. In order to improve the taste, marinate meat for not more than 24 hours.

INGREDIENTS: 1 quart buttermilk • 3 bay leaves • 3 cloves • 1 teaspoon peppercorns • 1 bundle chopped soup greens • 4 stalks thyme • 1 chemically untreated diced lemon

PREPARATION: Mix all ingredients, pour over the meat and marinade for not more than 2 days. If there is more than 26 ozs of meat, increase buttermilk and spices correspondingly.

Red Wine Marinade

INGREDIENTS: 1 bottle of red Burgundy • 4 chopped shallots • 2 chopped carrots • 1 teaspoon peppercorns • 5 juniper berries • 3 cloves • 2 bay leaves • peel of 1 chemically untreated lemon • peel of 1 chemically untreated orange • 1 stalk of thyme • 1 teaspoon sugar • 1 teaspoon salt

PREPARATION: Bring all ingredients to a boil, then cool down. Marinate 2 lbs beef in it for 24 hours. Use the marinade to pour over roasting meat and to prepare sauce.

Red Wine and Vinegar Marinade

INGREDIENTS: 1 bottle red wine • 2 tablespoons vinegar
Surig essence • 3 tablespoons sunflower oil • 2 chopped
onions • 1 tablespoon coriander seeds • 2 bay leaves
• 1 teaspoon peppercorns • 1 teaspoon juniper berries •
2 star anise seed • 1 cinnamon stalk

PREPARATION: Bring red wine, vinegar and 1 cup water
with all ingredients to boil once and cool down. Marinate
about 1¾ lb beef or game in it for 1–2 days. Use the marinade passed through a sieve to pour over roasting meat
and to prepare sauces.

White Wine Marinade

INGREDIENTS: 2 cups white wine • 4–5 tablespoons vinegar
essence • 3 oz sliced onion • 10 crushed juniper berries •
1 teaspoon mustard seeds • 1 teaspoon coriander seeds • 1 teaspoon peppercorns •
2 bay leaves • 1 tablespoon sugar

PREPARATION: Mix white wine and the
same quantity of water and all the remaining ingredients. Marinate about 2 lbs.
light meat or roast herrings in it for 1–2
days. Use the marinade passed through
a sieve to prepare sauce.

Spicy Marinade with Fir Tree Aroma

INGREDIENTS: 2 cups red wine • 2 cups red wine vinegar • 1 bundle chopped greens • 2 chopped onions • 3 bay leaves • 3 cloves • 10 crushed juniper berries • 1 chopped red chili pepper • 3½ oz mustard seeds • 1 tablespoon salt • 2 small, young fir tree twigs • 1 teaspoon cherry liquor

PREPARATION: Bring to boil red wine and vinegar with 2 cups water. Mix in all ingredients and cool down. Pour the marinade over 2 lbs pork neck or beef and marinate in a refrigerator for 7–8 days. Use the marinade passed through a sieve to prepare sauce.

Barbecue Marinade

INGREDIENTS: 3 tablespoons honey • 2 tablespoons sugar • 1 teaspoon vinegar essence Surig • 2 cups ketchup • 1 teaspoon brandy • 1 tablespoon Worcestershire sauce • 2–3 garlic cloves • 1 teaspoon marjoram • 1 teaspoon oregano • 1 teaspoon salt • 1 teaspoon curry powder • fresh ground pepper • cayenne pepper to taste.

PREPARATION: Melt honey and 2 tablespoons water and sugar. Mix with the other ingredients. brush on 2 lb cutlets, steaks or spare ribs and marinate in a well-covered vessel for 1 day. Prepare on grill.

Herb Marinade

INGREDIENTS: 1 cup medium dry white wine • 3 cups white wine vinegar • 4 peeled sliced garlic cloves • 2 chopped red chili peppers • ½ sliced fennel root • 1 thick cubed carrot • 1 bundle of sliced spring onion • 3 pieces of orange peel from 1 chemically untreated fruit • 1 bundle of thyme cut in big pieces • 4 stalks of rosemary cut in big pieces • 1 bundle of basil cut in strips • 1 tablespoon salt • 1 tablespoon sugar • 1 cup olive oil

> **TIP**
> This marinade is good to marinade chicken breast, rump steaks, cutlets and tuna fish.

PREPARATION: Boil wine and vinegar. Add everything except for oil, bring to boil, cool down. Mix with oil and marinate about 2 lb vegetables in it (cleaned pepper, tomatoes cut in halves, fennel, aubergine, zucchini, onion) for 2–3 days or 2 lb fish for 1 day.

Asian Marinade

INGREDIENTS: 4 chopped garlic cloves • 1 tablespoon chopped lemon grass • 1 chopped red chili pepper • 1 tablespoon grated ginger • 12 tablespoons soy sauce • 2 tablespoons oyster sauce • 6 tablespoons sunflower oil • 4 tablespoons honey • 4 tablespoons dry sherry

PREPARATION: Mix all ingredients well. Marinate about 1.5 lbs of meat or fish in it for 1–2 days depending on its thickness. Dry well, slice and roast or grill.

Sauces for Meat & Poultry

What would juicy roast pork, spicy beef olive or crisp duck right out of the oven be without sauce? There are usually enough drippings from big portions of roast to make sauce. Nevertheless, we will show you how to concoct exquisite sauces from meat juices and a variety of fine ingredients. Some of you wish to make a special sauce to go with steaks, schnitzels, meat rissoles, smoked pork, and quail or chicken wings. In this chapter we will tell you the best recipes for such fine sauces as Tomato Cognac Sauce and Calvados Apple Sauce. Can you guess what meals go with Plum Sauce, Bread Sauce, Leek Cream Sauce and Olive Thyme Butter? We guarantee that you will be surprised!

Beer Sauce with Roast Pork

TIP
Roast pork is delicious when served cold and sliced with bread and cream or apple horse radish (see 24). It is therefore advisable to put a bigger roast in the oven.

INGREDIENTS: 2 tablespoons butter • 2 tablespoons flour • 3 lbs roast pork with rind • 4 tablespoons sunflower oil • salt • freshly ground pepper • 2 garlic cloves • 5 spice cloves • 2 carrots • ½ celery root • 2 sticks leek • 1 parsley root • 2 onions • 2 tablespoons tomato paste • 2 bay leaves • ½ stick cinnamon • 1 bottle dark beer • honey

PREPARATION: Cream butter with flour and cool, Preheat oven to 374°F. Brush pork rind with a little oil. Spice the roast meat with salt and pepper. Cut the garlic into small pieces. Stick garlic together with cloves into the rind. Heat oil in roasting pan and roast meat until golden brown on the rind side. Clean vegetables, peel and cut into cubes. Turn meat and roast on opposite side. Pour 1 cup of hot water on meat and put roast in oven. Braise 1 hour, adding hot water if necessary. Pour vegetables and tomato paste over meat and braise together briefly. Combine bay leaves, one cinnamon stick and beer. Roast, periodically pouring gravy over meat. Remove roast meat, pour vegetables and meat juice through strainer. Turn temperature up to 410° F and put meat back into oven until crust is crisp. Stir flour-butter mixture into gravy piece by piece until thick. Season to taste.

Olive Pepper Sauce with Roast Pork

INGREDIENTS: 2 lbs roast pork roll • salt • freshly ground pepper • paprika • 4 tablespoons olive oil • 1 cup red wine • 2 red peppers • 2 garlic cloves • ½ cup Crème Fraîche • dark starch sauce • chili powder • 5 green olives and 5 black olives • 1 teaspoon fresh thyme leaves • 1 teaspoon lemon strips

TIP
Don't roast this meat too much or the pepper powder gets burnt and adds a bitter taste.

PREPARATION: Brush roll roast all over with a mixture of salt, pepper and paprika. Heat olive oil in a roasting pan (not too hot!) and roast the meat gently but thoroughly. Pour red wine over and simmer in a covered pot for 15 minutes. Turn the roast over, pour 1 cup of hot water over it. Clean, wash and cut pepper pods into small pieces. Peel and chop garlic finely. Add both to the meat during next 15 minutes. Cook the roll roast for a total of 60–70 minutes. Wrap the meat in aluminium foil. Purée the sauce and pour it through a fine strainer. Stir in Crème Fraîche. If desired, combine the sauce with sauce starch, season it with salt and chili powder. Cut olives into oblong, thin strips. Mix thyme and strips together into the sauce. Best served with wide pasta (noodles) and a side dish of green beans, cherry tomatoes and artichoke hearts.

Lime Sauce with Pork Medallions

INGREDIENTS: 1 lb pork fillet • 1 teaspoon Maggi spice mixture • 2 tablespoons sunflower oil • 1 chopped onion • ½ cup cream • 1 spoonful bouillon granules • 4 tablespoons sauce starch for light sauces • 1 lime • cayenne pepper • honey

PREPARATION: Skin, wash and dry the meat. Cut into slices 1 inch thick. Brush the medallions with spice mixture and roast them on both sides in hot oil. Wrap the medallions in foil. Cook onion in the drippings. Dissolve the roast grounds with 1 cup water. Stir together cream and granulated bouillon and let boil. Combine with sauce starch. Wash lime in hot water, dry it and peel off a little skin into

the sauce. Press the fruit out and season the sauce with lime juice, chili powder and honey. Warm the medallions in the sauce for a short time.

Serve with wild rice and sugar pea husks dipped in butter.

Lime Tomato Sauce with Meatballs

INGREDIENTS: 2 bread rolls • 1 cup lukewarm milk •
1 onion • 6 sage leaves • 1 tablespoon small capers •
2 lbs vine-tomatoes • 1 tablespoon butter • 1 lb of ground
veal • 1 egg • 1 tablespoon flour • salt • freshly ground
pepper • roasting fat • 4 tablespoons port wine •
1–2 dashes Tabasco • 4 tablespoons olive oil •
1 tablespoon lime juice

PREPARATION: Soak rolls in milk. Peel onion and cut
it into fine cubes. Chop sage. Plunge tomatos in boiling water, peel, core and quarter them. Cut the tomato quarters into small cubes. Heat butter in a pan,
cook the onion. Press out the rolls, tear them into
small pieces and put into the pan for a short time.
Then place it all in a dish. Add the ground meat, egg,
flour, sage and capers to the dish and mix it all well.
Season with salt and pepper. Form small balls out of
the meat mixture. Heat the roasting fat in a big pan,
fry the meatballs on both sides until they turn brown.
Put the fried meatballs in a dish and pour port wine
over them. Purée the tomato cubes in a mixer at the
highest speed. Season with salt, Tabasco sauce, olive
oil and lime juice. Serve the tomato sauce cold or warm with
the meat balls.

TIP

Both the ground meatballs
and the Lime Tomato Sauce
can be served cold or warm. It
is worthwhile, for a buffet, not
to make the balls too big and
to serve them on a plate of
smooth parsley. Have tooth
picks ready. Serve the sauce in
a small dish next to them.

Horseradish Red Beet Sauce with Pork Loaf

INGREDIENTS: 1 toasted roll • 2 lbs ground pork • 1 bunch spring onions • salt • freshly ground pepper • 2 table-spoons fresh marjoram leaves • 2 eggs • 2 tablespoons Dijon mustard • 1 bacon rind • 1 bunch soup greens • 2 bay leaves • 1 lb boiled beetroot • 3 ½ tablespoons grated horseradish • 5 oz Crème Fraiche • sugar • lemon juice • 5 oz whipped cream

PREPARATION: Soak roll in water, press out liquid, mash in bowl. Add meat. Chop lower half of onions finely, reserve tops. Mix onions, spices, egg and mushroom into meat, form into loaf. Heat oven to 200sF. Place bacon rind on bottom of baking pan, place meatloaf on it. Bake uncovered 20 minutes. Add finely chopped soup greens, basil leaves and 1 cup water, cover and bake another 40 minutes. Uncover last 15 minutes of baking. Wrap meat in aluminum foil and strain drippings. Grate ⅓ cup beets finely and reserve. Slice the rest and add to sauce. Mix grated beets with cream, horseradish, salt, sugar and lemon juice. Fold in whipped cream and sprinkle with chipped onion tops. Good with roast new potatoes.

Hunter's Sauce with Pork Steaks

INGREDIENTS: 4 pork steaks • salt • freshly ground pepper • 2 tablespoons baking fat • 2 tablespoons red port wine • 1 cup cream • 1 package Maggi Hunter Sauce • 2 tablespoons stewed cranberries

PREPARATION: Wash the steaks, dry them and brush all over with salt and pepper. Heat baking fat in a pan and roast the steaks on both sides. Preheat the oven to 400°F. Place the steaks one beside the other in an ovenproof dish. Dissolve roast grounds with port wine. Mix cream with Hunter Sauce, meat juice and stewed cranberries. Pour the Hunter Sauce over the steaks and roast for 20–25 minutes. Freshly made noodles, forest mushrooms or mushrooms fried in butter are suitable accompaniments.

Sherry Honey Marinade for Spare Ribs

INGREDIENTS: 3 lbs spare-ribs, divided into portions • 2 cloves garlic • 1 shallot • ½ cup sunflower oil • 7 tablespoons dry Sherry • 2 tablespoons oregano • 1 teaspoon sugar • 1 teaspoon salt • freshly ground pepper • 5 tablespoons honey

PREPARATION: Wash the spare ribs, dry them and place in a flat, wide dish to marinate. Peel and chop garlic cloves and shallots finely. Mix them with oil, sherry, oregano, sugar, salt and pepper. Pour the marinade over the ribs and turn the ribs over in it several times. Cover the dish with a cover or foil and put aside to cool. Let the ribs absorb the marinade for at least 24 hours. Save the marinade and put the ribs on a grill (not very near the heat!) and let them grill slowly. Turn them over several times, brushing on the saved marinade. After about 15 minutes, brush the ribs with honey and grill for 15 minutes more until a nice crust forms. Serve the ribs with a baguette and salad.

Mango Sauce with Spare-Ribs

INGREDIENTS: 1 cup Crème Fraîche • 3 tablespoons mango chutney • dash of highly concentrated vinegar • ½ teaspoon curry • salt • freshly ground pepper

DIRECTIONS FOR PREPARATION: Mix Crème Fraîche with chutncy, vinegar-essence and curry. Season with salt and pepper.

Marinated Spare Ribs

INGREDIENTS: 2 lbs spare ribs divided into portions • 6 tablespoons soy sauce • 1 teaspoon chopped ginger • 1 teaspoon chopped chili pepper • ½ teaspoon salt • 2 tablespoons honey • salt

PREPARATION: Put the meat in a flat dish. Mix soy sauce with ginger, salt and honey. Brush the spare ribs on both sides with it and marinate for 1–2 hours. Then grill for 10–15 minutes.

Tomato-Pineapple Dip with Pork Cutlets

INGREDIENTS: 1 chopped garlic clove • 1 teaspoon olive oil • 1 packet stuffed tomatoes • 1 can cut pineapple • 1 teaspoon Sambal oelek • salt • dash of highly concentrated vinegar

PREPARATION: Saute the garlic in hot oil for a short time. Add tomatoes and cook until creamy. Stir in drained pieces of pineapple, Samba oleic, salt and vinegar essence and let cool.

Fancy Sauce for Chicken Wings

INGREDIENTS: 3 lbs chicken wings • 8 tablespoons sunflower oil • 6 tablespoons soy sauce • salt • freshly ground pepper • 1 bottle tomato ketchup • 1 bottle curry sauce • 1 bottle sweet and sour chili sauce

PREPARATION: Wash the meat and dry it. Mix oil, soy sauce, salt and pepper together and brush the meat all over with it. Spread the wings on a baking sheet and let roast at 356°F for 1 hour. Mix the three sauces in a big dish and add the hot meat to it.
A crispy baguette tastes nice with this.

Plum Sauce with Stuffed Roast Pork Loin

INGREDIENTS: 2 ½ lbs pork loin, in one piece, deboned • salt • freshly ground pepper • 2 bunches spring onions • 1 apple • 4 tablespoons butter • 1 teaspoon chopped ginger • 2 tablespoons ground almonds • 2 tablespoons sunflower oil • 1 stick thyme • 2 bay leaves • 7 oz pitted prunes without stones • 1 cup red port wine • lemon juice • cinnamon • ground cloves

TIP
You can pierce the ready-bought pork loin with a wood skewer and stuff it. The hole for stuffing should not be too small.

PREPARATION: Wash the meat, dry it and cut into a rectangular shape. Sprinkle with salt and pepper. Clean spring onions and cut into small pieces. Quarter, peel, core and cut the apple into small cubes. Braise both the onions and the apple cubes in hot butter until they are soft. Mix with ginger, almonds, salt and pepper. Spread the stuffing onto the meat, roll it and tie it all together. Heat oil and thoroughly roast the meat. Pour thyme and bay leaves with 2 cups hot water over the meat and braise for 50 minutes. Turn the meat, add prunes and port wine and braise 15–20 minutes. Wrap the meat in foil. Remove thyme and bay leaves. Purée the gravy and add a little water, if necessary. Season with salt, pepper, lemon juice, cinnamon and clove powder.
Serve and rice with a lot of roasted almond sticks.

Cranberry Sauce with False Roast Wild Boar

TIP
The cranberry sauce can be stored in a jar for 3-4 months.

INGREDIENTS: 1 cup red wine • 1 cup red wine vinegar • 2 cubed onions • 2 peeled cloves of garlic • 3 bay leaves • 1 tablespoon crushed pepper grains • 1 tablespoon of crushed juniper berries • 1 teaspoon allspice • 3 cloves • 1 star-anise • 1 stick cinnamon • 1 bunch of thyme • 1 teaspoon sugar • 1 teaspoon salt • 1 non-treated orange in slices • 2½ lbs pork neck without bone • 4 tablespoons sunflower oil • 1 bunch cubed soup vegetables • 1 lb cranberries • 1 cup sugar • ½ cup Crème Fraîche • 1 piece fresh horseradish

PREPARATION: Boil red wine, vinegar and 1 cup water with onions, garlic, spices, sugar, salt and orange slices, then pour it over the meat. Allow the meat 2 days to absorb liquid. Dry the meat and brush it with salt and pepper. Pour the marinade through a strainer. Roast meat thoroughly in hot oil. Add the soup vegetables and half of the marinade and braise for 70–80 minutes. Turn the meat often and continue to add marinade. Mix the washed cranberries with sugar and let boil for 3 minutes. Wrap the meat in foil. Pour the gravy through a strainer, boil, mix with 5 tablespoons cranberries and Crème Fraîche, season with salt and pepper and grate a little horseradish into the sauce. Delicious with Czech yeast dumplings.

Malt Sauce with Smoked Pork

INGREDIENTS: 2 lbs raw smoked pork without bones • 1 lb carrots • ¾ cup vegetable bouillon • ½ cup malt beer • 2–3 tablespoons Mondamin roast broth • 3 teaspoons dark Fix-Sauce Thickener • 2 tablespoons Crème Fraîche • salt • freshly ground pepper

PREPARATION: Wash and dry the meat. Preheat the oven to 400°F. Put the smoked pork and the hot water in a roasting pan. Braise meat covered in the oven for 15 minutes. Clean, peel and cut the carrots into big pieces. Add the carrots and bouillon to the meat and cook for 20 minutes. Remove the cover and let the smoked pork brown for 15 minutes. Wrap the meat in foil. Put malt beer and roast broth in a pot and let boil. Thicken the sauce with a sauce thickener, soften it with Crème Fraîche and season with salt and pepper.

Serve with creamy potato purée or buttery, slightly browned noodles.

Apricot Sauce with Smoked Pork

INGREDIENTS: 3 lbs raw smoked pork with bone • ½ cup chicken broth • 3 tablespoons apricot nectar • 4 tablespoons maple syrup • 4 tsp of brandy • 1 large can apricot halves • 3 tablespoons soy suace • 3 teaspoons highly concentrated vinegar • salt • freshly ground pepper

PREPARATION: Wash and dry the meat. Preheat the oven to 400°F. Put the smoked pork in a roasting pot and pour hot chicken broth over it. Braise in a covered pot for 60 minutes.

Combine apricot nectar with 1 tablespoon maple syrup and brandy and stir together. Brush smoked pork several times with mixture during roasting. Take meat out and wrap in foil. To make a sauce, purée the apricots in their juice, mix with soy sauce, vinegar essence maple syrup. Season with salt and pepper. Slice smoked pork, sprinkle it with roast broth and serve apricot sauce on the side. Serve with Asian Mie-Noodles or rich, aromatic Basmati-Rice.

Bread Sauce with Pork in Milk

INGREDIENTS: 2 lbs pork • salt • freshly ground pepper • freshly ground caraway • 4 tablespoons fat • 2 chopped shallots • 2 chopped cloves of garlic • 7 oz sliced brown mushrooms • 4 cups hot milk • 3 bay leaves • 2 sticks thyme • 6 slices toasted bread • 1 spoonful chicken sauce base (Lacroix) • 1 teaspoon anchovy paste • a little grated lemon peel • 4 tablespoons chopped parsley

TIP
To make the sauce smooth, purée the roast broth with shallots, garlic and mushrooms. This way, you will need less bread to thicken the sauce.

PREPARATION: Wash and dry the meat and brush with salt, pepper and caraway powder. Heat roasting fat and thoroughly roast the meat for 15 minutes. Add shallots, cloves of garlic and mushrooms to the meat and pour 2 cups of hot milk over it. Put bay leaves and stick of thyme in milk. Add the rest of the milk after about 30 minutes. Cook the roast for the whole of 70-80 minutes, constantly turning the meat. Wrap the meat in foil. Remove crusts from bay leaves and thyme. Remove the toasted bread and cut it into cubes. Dissolve them in the roast broth while stirring. Season with chicken sauce base, anchovy paste, pepper, lemon peel and parsley.
Serve with vegetable plate of carrots, celery sticks, broccoli, asparagus and kohlrabi.

Sauerkraut Sauce and Pea Sauce with Knuckle of Pork

INGREDIENTS: 3 lbs fresh pork knuckle • salt • 1 bunch of cubed soup vegetables • 1 teaspoon pepper grains • 3 bay leaves • 1 bunch spring onions • 6 tablespoons butter • 1 cup frozen peas • 2 oz bacon • 7 oz sauerkraut • 1 peeled and cubed apple • 1 cup cream • 1 teaspoon pepper powder • freshly ground pepper

TIP
Both sauces are also delicious with spit-roasted leg or saddle of piglet.

PREPARATION: Wash the meat and put it into a big pot. Fill with cold water and boil with salt, the soup vegetables, pepper and bay leaves for 2–3 hours until the meat is well done. Clean and cut spring onions in small pieces. Braise in 2 tablespoons butter until they are soft. Boil the peas in 2 cups salted water until they are soft, drain, purée with spring onions and press through a strainer. Refine with a little butter.

Cut the bacon into very small cubes, roast it in the rest of the butter, add sauerkraut, apple cubes and a little cooking water and cook for 20 minutes. Purée the sauerkraut and strain. Stir the pea and sauerkraut purées with a little cream, mix the sauerkraut sauce with pepper powder, and season both sauces with salt and pepper.
Serve with small roast or boiled potatoes.

Dark Bread Sauce with Sauerbraten

INGREDIENTS: 2 lbs shoulder of beef • 4 tablespoons sunflower oil • ½ cup pear juice • ⅓ cup red wine • ¾ cup vegetable broth • 1 bag of Instant Fix for Sweet-Sour Roast • 1 slice of dark bread • 1 big pear • 1 teaspoon sugar • 1 tablespoon butter • 4 teaspoons pear brandy • 2 tablespoons maple syrup

PREPARATION: Wash and dry the meat. Briefly roast it in hot oil. Preheat the oven to 400°F. Stir pear juice, red wine and vegetable broth together with Instant fix for Sweet-Sour Roast. Crumble the bread slice and stir into broth. Pour it all around the meat. Cook the meat in a closed pot in the oven for 70–80 minutes. Peel, core and cut the pear into thin segments. Melt sugar into light caramel and add pear segments, butter, pear brandy and maple syrup. Wrap the meat in foil. Mix the gravy with a mixer and stir the pear sauce into it.

Tasty with bread dumplings and broccoli florets, garnished with butter and almonds.

Mango Chili Sauce with False Loin Cooked in a Clay Pot

TIP
The piquant preparation in a baked clay pot can be used for the same amount of raw smoked pork instead of false loin.

INGREDIENTS: 2 lbs false loin • salt • freshly ground pepper • 1 teaspoon curry • 2 orange slices • 1 lemon slices • 2 bay leaves • 2 ripe mangos • 2 peeled garlic cloves • 1 tablespoon lemon juice • 2 tablespoons orange juice • 2 tablespoons soy sauce • 1 teaspoon chopped ginger • 1 teaspoon dried thyme • 1 red chopped chili pepper pod • 4 tablespoons sunflower oil • 1 bag of Instant Fix for Roast Beef

PREPARATION: Wash and dry the meat. Rub with salt, pepper and curry. Cover with citrus slices and bay leaves. Fill the clay pot with water according to the instructions. Peel the mangos, remove the pitts and cut them finely into cubes. Put 4 tablespoons cubes aside. Purée the rest with garlic, lemon and orange juice, soy sauce and ginger. Stir in thyme, chili pepper pod, sunflower oil, 1 cup water and Instant Fix. Put the meat in the clay pot and pour the sauce over it. Cook at 400°F for 100 minutes. Wrap the meat in foil. Mix the meat juice with a mixer, season with salt and pepper and stir in mango cubes.

Rice with non-salty pistachio nuts and cilantro is excellent with this dish.

Burgundy Sauce with Boiled Beef or Ox with Horseradish

INGREDIENTS: 2 lbs boiled beef or ox with horseradish • 2 tablespoons roasting fat • salt • freshly
ground pepper • 1 bottle of red Burgundy • 6 sprigs
thyme • 3 bay leaves • 6 crushed juniper berries •
1 teaspoon crushed pepper grains • 1 teaspoon allspice • 1 teaspoon fennel seeds • 1 big piece of
orange peel • 3 peeled garlic cloves • 4 red onions
• 7 oz small mushrooms • 4 tablespoons butter •
dark sauce thickener

TIP
The meat gets a special
spicy flavor if it sits in the
red wine for a few hours.

PREPARATION: Wash the meat, dry it and cut in 4 cm
large cubes. Heat roasting fat and roast the meat all
over in it. Sprinkle with salt and pepper. Add red
wine, thyme, bay leaves, juniper, pepper, allspice,
fennel, orange peel and garlic. Cook the meat in
a covered pot for 70–80 minutes. In the meantime,
peel the onions and cut them oblong into thin strips.
Clean mushrooms. Cook the onions and mushrooms
in hot butter until soft. Take the meat cubes out of the
meat juice and strain the gravy. Thicken it slightly
with sauce thickener. Stir in meat cubes, mushrooms
and onions and season with salt and pepper. Serve
with white bread or "Spätzle" (noodles) and juicy red
cabbage.

Marinated Beef Fillet

INGREDIENTS: 1 lb beef fillet • 6 tablespoons Marsala (Sicilian sweet red wine) • 6 tablespoons soy sauce • 1 tablespoon starch • 1 small piece fresh ginger root • 2 garlic cloves • 4 small onions • ¾ cup mushrooms • 2 tablespoons oil • salt • freshly ground pepper • 1 table-spoon sesame seeds

PREPARATION: Cut the beef fillet into thin strips. Stir Marsala, soy sauce and starch together in a small dish, pour over the meat and let sit for 30 minutes. Peel and chop ginger finely. Peel and cut garlic cloves and onions into fine slices. Clean and quarter mushrooms. Heat oil, remove beef from the marinade and, while stirring, brown it briefly at high heat for 3 minutes. Add ginger garlic, onions, and mushrooms and sauté briefly. Pour the marinade over it and let everything simmer for 3 more minutes. Season with salt and pepper. Roast sesame seeds in a small pan. Arrange meat with sauce, sprinkle with sesame and serve with curry rice.

Rose-Hip Sauce with Roast Beef

INGREDIENTS: 2 lbs beef leg • salt • freshly ground pepper • 1 teaspoon dried thyme • 5 oz fat bacon in thin slices • 2 tablespoons oil • 1 bag of Instant Fix for Sour Roast (sweet-sour flavor) • 1 teaspoon Hubertus (Ubena) wild spices • 3 tablespoons rose-hip jam • 4 tablespoons cream

PREPARATION: Wash the meat and dry it. Rub with salt, pepper and thyme. Cover the roast with bacon and wrap with kitchen twine. Heat oil in a pan and roast the meat thoroughly until there is a brown crust. Pour over 2 cups hot water and stir Fix For Sweet-Sour Roast and wild spices into it. Braise the roast in a covered pot at medium heat for 90 minutes. Remove the cover and cook for another 30 minutes. Take the meat out and wrap it in foil. Stir rose-hip jam and cream into the sauce. Season with salt and pepper once again. Remove the bacon and slice the meat.

Serve with potato dumplings and cabbage, stewed in butter.

Madeira Sauce with Beef Tongue

INGREDIENTS: 1 beef tongue • salt • 1 tablespoon pepper • 1 teaspoon allspice • 3 cloves • 2 pieces of star-anise • ½ cinnamon stick • 2 bay leaves • 2 chopped onions • 1 bunch soup vegetables cubed • 4 sticks thyme • 1 piece of lemon peel • 3 tablespoons butter • 2 cubed onions • 3 teaspoons flour • freshly ground pepper • sugar • lemon juice • 8 tablespoons of Madeira (Spanish dessert wine)

PREPARATION: Wash the tongue and let it boil in salty water for 2 hours. Then add pepper, allspice, cloves, star-anise, cinnamon stick, bay leaves, onions, soup vegetables, thyme and lemon peel and cook the mixture 60–90 minutes or until the meat is tender. Then immediately hold the tongue under a stream of cold water and take off the skin. Boil the broth down to 2 ½ cups and strain. Heat butter and braise the onions until they are soft. Stir in flour and roast until light brown. Add the broth gradually and let the sauce simmer for 10 minutes. Strain it and season with salt, pepper, sugar, lemon juice and Madeira wine. Slice the tongue and heat it in the Madeira sauce.

Serve with mashed potatoes, sweet chestnuts and carrots with raisins and almonds.

TIP

Salted tongue should be soaked for 8 hours and cooked in water without salt. Cooled, thin slices of tongue are delicious served on bread with creamy horseradish sauce (see 24).

Tarragon Cream Sauce with Beef Roulades

INGREDIENTS: 2 tablespoons butter • 2 tablespoons flour • 1 teaspoon dried tarragon • 4 beef fillets • salt • pepper • tarragon mustard • 8 slices bacon • 1 chopped onion • 4 small salted cucumbers • 4 bay leaves • 4 tablespoons roasting fat • 2 cups meat broth • 1 bunch soup vegetables in cubes • ⅔ cups red wine • ½ cup Crème Fraîche • 2 sticks fresh tarragon

PREPARATION: Knead butter with flour and tarragon and set aside to cool. Spread the meat out, sprinkle it with salt and pepper and brush with mustard. Cover it with 2 bacon slices and sprinkle with onion cubes. Put a pickle (gherkin) on the thin side and bay leaves on the wide side of meat slice. Roll the meat from the thin side up and tie together with wood skewer, olive pins or cooking string.

Heat roasting fat in a pan and let the roulades roast. Pour the meat broth over them and braise for 60 minutes. Put the soup vegetables in between the roulades and pour red wine over them. Braise for 50–60 minutes or until the meat is tender. Wrap the meat in foil, strain the gravy and boil it. Put the meat back in the sauce and sprinkle with tarragon leaves. Serve with boiled potatoes and cauliflower sprinkled with a mixture of breadcrumbs and hot butter.

Asparagus Cream with Beef Fillet

INGREDIENTS: 2 lbs white asparagus • salt • 1 pinch of sugar • 2 tablespoons butter • 1 tablespoon flour • 1 cup cream • freshly ground pepper • 4 tablespoons chopped parsley • 1 bunch spring onions • 7 oz brown mushrooms • 3 tomatoes • 4 slices beef fillet at 5 oz each • 1 tablespoon roasting fat

PREPARATION: Peel the asparagus and remove the stringy ends. Cut into 1 inch pieces, cook in boiling salted water together with sugar and 1 teaspoon of butter for 10 minutes until soft. Remove and drain. Heat 1 tablespoons butter, cook flour in it, add the asparagus broth while stirring, and boil. Stir in cream, season with salt and pepper. Add parsley and asparagus and let simmer at low heat.

Clean spring onions and cut them into small pieces. Wash, clean and quarter the mushrooms. Scald tomatoes. Peel off the skin, remove the stems and cut into coarse cubes. Sauté onions, mushrooms and tomatoes in the butter. Spice with salt and pepper. Wash the beef fillet, dry it, season with salt and pepper and brown on both sides in hot roasting fat. Arrange in portions and add the asparagus cream and mushroom mixture.

Tomato Cognac Sauce with Beef Steaks

INGREDIENTS: 2 shallots • ½ bunch parsley • 4 big tomatoes • 1 tablespoon olive oil • 2 tablespoons butter • 8 beef steaks, each 3½ oz • salt • freshly ground pepper • 4 tablespoons Cognac • 1 tablespoon Worcestershire Sauce • 1 cup beef broth

> **TIP**
> This fine sauce is also suitable for meatballs, made from lean minced beef, egg, mustard and some thyme.

PREPARATION: Peel and slice shallots finely. Clean and chop chives. Put tomatoes into hot water, cut off stems, peel off skin and chop coarsely. Heat butter and olive oil in a pan, season steaks with salt and pepper. Cook quickly at high heat, but not completely. Remove steaks from pan and let stand in warm place. Remove pan from fire, pour out excess fat, put the cognac in the pan, set on fire and put back onto range until fire goes out. Let the shallots simmer in the pan until soft. Stir in the tomatoes, Worcestershire sauce, meat juice, salt, and pepper and bring to a boil. Put the steaks in the sauce and simmer. Put finished steaks onto a plate, let sauce thicken, add some chives and pour on steaks.

Rice and pasta with brown butter, go well with this dish.

Herb Sour Cream for Roast Beef

TIP
The cooking time per half inch or centimeter of roast beef is approximately 8 minutes. Roast Beef is available at the butcher shop and can be bought pre-cooked. Have the meat cut into thin slices at the shop.

INGREDIENTS: 1½ lb Roast Beef • 10 tablespoons roasting fat • salt • freshly ground pepper • 1 hard-boiled egg • 1¾ cups sour cream • 4 tablespoons mayonnaise • 6–8 tablespoons pickle juice • 1 teaspoon honey • 1 pickle • 1 peeled shallot • 1 peeled clove of garlic • 2 tablespoons capers • 2 anchovy filets • 2 tablespoons hot mustard • 1 cup chopped herbs (parsley, chervil, dill, chives, rugola)

PREPARATION: Wash and dry meat, and lay fatty side down in a roasting pan. Heat the roasting fat and pour over the meat. Let simmer at medium heat for 50–60 minutes. Season the roast beef all over with salt and pepper and let cool. Shell egg and cut in cubes. Mix the sour cream with mayonnaise, pickle juice and honey until smooth. Chop the pickle, shallot, garlic and capers into very fine pieces. Wash anchovy filets with cold water and dab dry. Then chop finely. Add with mustard and chopped herbs to the mayonnaise mixture and stir. Salt and pepper. If desired, pour more pickle juice into mix. Slice cooled roast beef with a sharp knife or a meat slicer. Put the sour herb cream on the side.

Crispy fried potatoes go well with this meal.

Shallot Mustard Sauce for Beef Toast

INGREDIENTS: 6 peeled shallots • 2 tablespoons butter, sugar • 1½ tablespoons of cognac • 7 tablespoons veal broth • salt • freshly ground pepper • 1 teaspoon thyme leaf • 2 tablespoons Crème Fraîche • 1 tablespoon mayonnaise • 1 teaspoon hot mustard • 2 tomatoes • 4 beef fillets, 4 oz each • 8 slices toasted sandwich bread.

PREPARATION: Halve the shallots and slit them into strips. Melt one tablespoon butter over low heat until transparent and sprinkle with a pinch of sugar. Add cognac and veal broth. Let simmer lightly until the liquid is completely boiled away. Season with salt and pepper and refine with thyme. Stir the Crème Fraîche and mustard until smooth. Slice tomatoes thin. Salt and pepper beef filets and fry in butter for 2 minutes on each side. Spread the sauce onto 4 slices of bread. Cover with tomatoes, shallots, and cooked beef fillets and remaining bread slices.

Bacon Cheese Sauce with Steak Tartare on Bread

INGREDIENTS: 4 oz bacon • 1 cup cream • 1 teaspoon flour • 8 oz grated Gouda • salt • freshly ground pepper • freshly ground nutmeg • 1 cup steak tartare • 2 egg yolks • 4 tablespoons chopped onions • 2 tablespoons chopped pickles • 2 tablespoons chopped capers • Worcestershire sauce • 4 slices toasted bread

PREPARATION: Fry 4 slices of bacon until crispy. Dice finely the remaining bacon and fry until crisp. Stir in cream and flour let, thicken, and add the cheese. Season with salt,

pepper, and nutmeg. Switch the stove grill on. Mix steak tartare with egg yolks, onions, pikles and capers, season with salt, pepper and Worcestershire sauce. Spread the steak tartare on the bread slices and put in a large soufflé dish. Mix bacon cubes with the sauce, pour over the bread slices, and bake until golden yellow. Put one bacon slice onto each slice of toasted bread.

Endive salad with apple and pikles goes well with this.

Dill Sauce with Boiled Veal

INGREDIENTS: ¾ cups veal • salt • 1 halved onion • 3 bay leaves • 1 teaspoon mustard seeds • 1 teaspoon whole allspice • 1 teaspoon coriander seeds • 1 teaspoon whole peppers • 1 bundle of soup vegetables, diced • 5 tablespoons butter • 4 tablespoons flour • 1 cup milk • ¾ cups cream • freshly ground pepper • lemon juice • Worcestershire sauce • freshly grated nutmeg • 2 bunches chopped dill

PREPARATION: Wash the meat and put in a pot with salted water, cover. Let simmer for 1 hour. Add onion, bay leaves, mustard seeds, allspice, coriander, pepper and soup vegetables and let simmer for 1 additional hour. Take the meat out and wrap it in aluminum foil. Reduce the stock to 3 cups. Heat the butter and lighty brown the flour in it. Add milk, cream, and the reduced stock and let simmer uncovered for 10 minutes. Season to taste with salt, pepper, lemon juice, Worcestershire sauce, and nutmeg. Finally, stir dill in.

Bohemian dumplings and assorted boiled vegetables go well with this.

Orange Ginger Sauce with Spring Meat Rolls

INGREDIENTS: 4 eggroll wrappers • 7 oz roast veal (sliced) • 7 oz roast beef in slices • 2 tablespoons oyster sauce • 4 tablespoons sweet soy sauce • 2 tablespoons soy sauce • 4 chopped garlic cloves • 4 spring onions in thin strips • 4 fresh Shiitake mushrooms in strips • 5 tablespoons soy sprouts • 3 red chopped chili peppers • 4 stalks cilantro • 1 carrot in thin strips • sunflower oil • ¾ cups orange juice • 1 tablespoon chopped ginger • 4 chopped shallots • 4 tablespoons tomato ketchup • 2 tablespoons honey • ½ teaspoon starch • lime juice

PREPARATION: Cut the veal and beef into thin strips. Mix oyster sauce, 2 tablespoons of the sweet soy sauce, the soy sauce, and half of the garlic and add it to the meat. Spread out 4 eggroll wrappers. Put spring onions, Shiitake mushrooms, soy sprouts, a little chili, cilantro green tops, and carrots lengthwise onto the wrappers and top with the meat. Turn up the sides and roll up. Fry in hot oil until crispy. Boil orange juice with ginger, the remaining garlic, shallots, chili, the remaining soy sauce, ketchup and honey for 10 minutes. Mix starch with a little cold water until smooth, add it to the sauce and let boil up once. Stir in 2 tablespoons of oil and season to taste with lime juice.

Porcini Sauce with Veal Rissoles

INGREDIENTS: 2 chopped shallots • 4 tablespoons butter • 4 slices toast bread • a bit of milk • 1 egg • 1 egg yolk • 1 teaspoon mustard • 1 teaspoon fresh thyme • 4 dried tomatoes in oil • 1 lb minced veal • salt • freshly ground pepper • 2 tablespoons butter • 1 oz dried porcini mushrooms • 2 red onions chopped • 1 chopped garlic clove • 1 cup cream • light sauce thickener • 2 tablespoons chopped parsley • 4 tablespoons whipped cream

PREPARATION: Braise shallots in 2 tablespoons butter until soft. Cut the crust off the bread, drip a little milk on it and then squeeze it well. Mix the bread, meat, egg yolk, mustard, thyme leaves and shallots. Blot oil from the tomatoes and dice finely. Add to meat mixture. Season with salt and pepper. Form 8 small, oval rissoles from the meat mixture and fry them in butter until golden brown. Soak the porcinis in 1 cup lukewarm water for 30 minutes. Braise onions and garlic in the remaining butter until soft. Add the porcini with the soaking water to it and let simmer uncovered for 10 more minutes. Purée the sauce with a hand mixer and, if desired, thicken it with a little sauce thickener. Finally, stir parsley and cream into it. Mashed potatoes go well with this dish.

TIP

It is advisable, before making the rissoles from the mince meat substance, to fry a little of it in some butter and taste. You can add spice if you desire.

Pizzaiola Sauce with Veal Cutlets

TIP
This typically Italian sauce tastes good with pork cutlets, pork schnitzels, or grilled fish.

INGREDIENTS: 4 veal cutlets • salt • freshly ground pepper • a little flour • 2 tablespoons butter • 6 tablespoons olive oil • 1 stalk rosemary • 2 stalks thyme • 1 lb fleshy tomatoes • 4 peeled garlic cloves • 2 peeled shallots • 3 tablespoons tomato purée • ⅔ cups red wine • 1 bay leaf • 4 green olives • fresh oregano leaves • Parmesan

PREPARATION: Wash and dry the meat. Season with salt and pepper and sprinkle with flour on both sides. Heat butter and 2 tablespoons oil, add rosemary and thyme to the pan and fry the schnitzels in the aromatic fat on both sides until golden brown. Dip tomatoes shortly into boiling water and skin them, cut off the stalks. Dice the tomatoes, garlic, and shallots finely. Sauté them in the remaining oil. Add ketchup, red wine, diced tomatoes and a bay leaf. Let the sauce simmer uncovered for about 15 minutes. Chop olives very finely. When the sauce has been reduced to a creamy consistency, season it to taste with salt and pepper. Remove the bay leaf. Add the olives and some oregano to the sauce. Pour Pizzaiola over the hot schnitzels and grate Parmesan on top.

Spicy Coconut Sauce with Veal Fillet and Pineapple

INGREDIENTS: 1⅓ lbs veal fillet • 2 tablespoons light soy sauce • 1 teaspoon freshly grated ginger • 1 peeled garlic • 1 baby pineapple • 1 tablespoon red curry paste • 2 cups coconut milk • juice of ½ lime • sugar • fish sauce • 2 tablespoons butter • 2 tablespoons peanut oil

PREPARATION: Cut the veal in 4 slices and spread with soy sauce, fresh ginger, and finely chopped garlic. Peel the baby pineapple and cut in 4 slices. Heat curry paste in a pot and stir with a little coconut milk until smooth. Add the remaining coconut milk and let simmer over low heat for 10 minutes while stirring constantly. Season to taste with lime juice, a dash of sugar, and fish sauce. Fry the pineapple slices in butter on both sides until golden brown and sprinkle with a little sugar. Grill in a preheated oven at 250 °F until caramelized. Brown the veal fillet slices in hot oil on both sides. Put the pineapple on the veal fillets and pour the coconut sauce over it.

Basmati rice is tasty with this dish.

Onion Raisin Sauce for Veal Liver

INGREDIENTS: 1¼ lbs veal liver • 1 lb white onions • 2 table-spoons olive oil • 1 stalk thyme • salt • sugar • flour • 2 tablespoons butter • freshly ground pepper • 2 tablespoons balm vinegar • 2 cups veal stock • 5 tablespoons raisins soaked in port wine • 5 table-spoons roasted pine nuts • 2 table-spoons chopped parsley

PREPARATION: Cut veal liver and onions in thin strips. Fry the onion in olive oil until golden brown, add thyme leaves and season to taste with salt and a little sugar. Strain onions through a strainer and collect the olive oil. Sprinkle veal liver strips slightly with flour. Heat 2 tablespoons butter and the collected olive in an oil-coated pan and fry the liver on both sides well in it. Season to taste with salt, pepper, and vinegar and add the veal stock. Add onion strips and let reduce a little. Finally, stir in drained raisins and pine nuts and garnish with parsley.

Creamy polenta goes well with it.

Caper Tomato Sauce with Veal Liver

INGREDIENTS: 4 slices veal liver • salt • freshly ground pepper • flour • 1 egg • 1 hard roll • 8–10 tablespoons butter • 2 garlic cloves • 2 onions • 2 oz Parma ham • 2 tablespoons olive oil • 2 cans tomatoes • 2 bay leaves • 1 teaspoon thyme leaves • 4 tablespoons tomato ketchup • 2 anchovies • 1 red chili pepper • 4 tablespoons small capers • 1 bundle of Rugola

PREPARATION: Cut the liver in strips. Spice with salt and pepper and roll in flour. Separate the egg, whisk the egg white until stiff and fold in the egg yolk. Grate the roll. Melt an ample amount of butter in frying pan. Coat the liver strips in egg and breadcrumbs. Fry in hot butter until crispy and absorb extra fat onto kitchen paper towel. Peel garlic cloves and onions, and dice. Cut the Parma ham in small pieces. Heat olive oil and fry garlic, onions and ham for a short time. Add tomatoes, bay leaves, thyme, and ketchup and boil uncovered until creamy consistency. Rinse the anchovies and chop them finely, cut chili in small pieces. Add both, together with capers, to the sauce and season to taste with pepper. Clean Rugola, wash it, and cut in strips. Stir into the sauce and serve with the liver strips.

Macaroni goes well with this dish.

Orange Onion Sauce with Veal Tripe

INGREDIENTS: 2 lbs veal tripe, parboiled by a butcher • 1 bundle of soup vegetables in cubes • 3 bay leaves • 1 onion • 3 allspice cloves • 1 teaspoon pimento seeds • 1 teaspoon ground pepper • salt • 4 tablespoons sugar • 4 tablespoons balsamic vinegar • 3 organic oranges • 1 organic lemon • 1 lb red onions • freshly ground pepper • 4 tablespoons cold butter

PREPARATION: Wash the tripe and cover them in a pot with water. Add soup vegetables, bay leaves, a halved onion, cloves, allspice, pepper, and salt and boil at a mild heat until soft. Take the livers out and cut them in thin strips. Strain the broth through a fine strainer and reduce to 2 cups. Melt the sugar to a light caramel. Add vinegar and the broth and reduce to one third. Wash 1 orange and the lemon in hot water and dry. Peel the skin of the both fruits with a peeler. Squeeze all the fruits out. Peel onions and cut them in fine strips. Add citrus juice, peel strips and onions to the broth and let simmer uncovered for 30 minutes. Heat the tripe in the sauce, season to taste with salt and pepper, and stir in butter in small pieces.

Rice goes well with this dish.

Mascarpone Mustard Sauce with Veal Heart

INGREDIENTS: 1½ lb veal heart • 1 quart meat broth •
2 peeled shallots • 1 peeled garlic clove •
4 tablespoons butter • 2 tablespoons flour •
6 oz mascarpone cheese • 2 tablespoons coarse
ground mustard • 1 tablespoon spicy mustard •
1 tablespoon sweet mustard • 1 tablespoon lemon
juice • 2 tablespoons orange juice • salt • freshly
ground pepper • 2 tablespoons chopped dill

TIP
Not only veal heart, but
also beef, chicken or turkey
heart taste good in this
sauce.

PREPARATION: Clean the meat, and cover in a pot with the
broth. Boil the heart until soft and take it out of the pot.
Reduce the broth to 2 cups. Cut the meat in bite-sized
pieces. Dice shallots and garlic very finely. Melt butter, fry
onions and garlic in it, add flour and let it brown lightly.
Add the broth and let simmer for 10 minutes. Stir in mascarpone, the various mustard sorts and citrus juices. Season
the sauce to taste with salt and pepper. Heat the heart in
the sauce and stir in dill.

Cranberry Port Wine Sauce with Venison

INGREDIENTS: 1¾ lbs boned shoulder of venison • salt • pepper • 2 tablespoons oil • 2 onions cut in small pieces • 2 peeled carrots • ½ peeled celery root • 8 juniper berries • 2 bay leaves • 5 whole peppercorns • 2 cloves • 5 all-spice berries • 2 tablespoons tomato purée • 1 bottle strong red wine • 3¼ cups game sauce base • 1 teaspoon starch • ½ cup red port wine • 3½ oz Chanterelles • 3 tablespoons butter • 1 chopped shallot • 7 tablespoons • nutmeg • 1 tablespoon chopped parsley • 2 slices toast • 4 tablespoons preserved cranberries

PREPARATION: Cut the meat in 3 centimeter pieces, season it, and fry well in oil. Add onions, vegetable, and spice and after about 5 minutes stir in tomato purée. Baste with 1 cup of red wine and let reduce completely. Repeat this process three times. Braise covered in an oven at 350 °F for about 2 hours, basting with the game sauce base from time to time. Take the meat out and pour the sauce through a fine strainer. Stir the starch with port wine and bind the sauce with it. Let simmer for about 10 minutes, and then put the meat in again. Clean the Chanterelles and fry them in 1 tablespoon of butter. Add the shallot and thicken with cream. Season to taste and garnish with parsley. Cut the toast bread into 1 inch long and ⅛ inch thick segments and fry in the remaining butter slowly until golden yellow. Serve the ragout with sauce, toast, and cranberries.

Rosemary Sauce with Leg of Hare

INGREDIENTS: 4 legs of hare • salt • 1 teaspoon whole peppercorns • 4 tablespoons butter • 1 bundle of soup vegetables in cubes • 1 chopped clove of garlic • 2 diced onions • 1¾ cups game sauce base • 1¾ cups red wine • 6 stalks rosemary • 1 tablespoon red currant jelly • 3½ oz cold butter • 3 tomatoes

PREPARATION: Skin the legs of hare, wash and dry them. Crust 1 teaspoon salt with the whole peppercorns finely in a mortar and rub the meat with it. Heat the butter in a frying pan and fry the meat well in it all over. Then pour game sauce base over it. After 30 minutes, add soup vegetables, a clove of garlic, and onions to the meat and braise a little. Add red wine, 5 stalks of rosemary, and braise for additional 30 minutes until soft. Wrap the meat in the aluminum foil, reduce the gravy to about 1 cup, and pour it through a strainer. Chop leaves from the remaining rosemary stalks finely and sprinkle them in the gravy, season with salt. Stir the butter in flakes into it. Dip tomatoes shortly into boiling water, skin, pit them, and dice finely. Mix with the sauce and pour over the legs of hare.

Porcini mushrooms braised in butter, and homemade noodles go well with this dish.

Juniper Cream with Hare Fillet

INGREDIENTS: 1 lb wild hare fillet • 20 juniper berries • salt • freshly ground pepper • 7 oz thinly sliced, smoked bacon • 2 tablespoons sunflower oil • 3 tablespoons gin • 1¾ cups game sauce base • 1 pear • 2 tablespoons butter • 1 cup Crème Fraîche

PREPARATION: Wash the meat and dry. Crush 6 juniper berries in a mortar and mix with salt and pepper. Rub the meat with it, wrap bacon around it and tie with kitchen string. Heat oil in a frying pan and brown the meat. Pour gin over it. Braise the meat for 5 minutes. Pour the game sauce base into it, crush the remaining juniper berries, and add them to the meat. Braise the meat uncovered for 15 minutes. Quarter the pears, peel, pit, and cut them in small cubes. Melt the butter and cook the pear cubes in it until soft. Take the meat out of the gravy, remove the bacon and wrap the meat in aluminum foil. Pour the sauce through a strainer. Stir Crème Fraîche and boil lightly until creamy. Season to taste with salt and pepper and stir the pears in. Heat the meat in the sauce.

Oyster mushrooms and small potatoes, both fried in butter, go well with this.

Marinated Wild Boar Leg

INGREDIENTS: 1 peeled onion • 1 bundle of soup vegetables in cubes • 4 lbs wild-boar leg without bones • 2 bay leaves • 2 stalks thyme • 1 stalk rosemary • 1 bottle red wine • ⅓ cup highly-concentrated vinegar • 4 tablespoons butter • salt • freshly ground pepper • juice and peel of 1 orange • 1 tablespoon bitter orange jam • ¾ cup cream • dark sauce thickener

PREPARATION: Cut the onion in thin rings. Wash the meat and put it in a bowl. Add onion rings, soup vegetables, bay leaves, 1 stalk thyme and rosemary and pour red wine and vinegar over it. Marinate the meat for 2–3 days, turning it frequently. Take the meat out of the marinade and dry it. Roast it all over in fried butter, season with salt and pepper. Strain the marinade. Braise the meat for 2½ to 3 hours. Baste continuously with the marinade and about ½ cup hot water. Take the meat out of the gravy and wrap it in an aluminum foil. Reduce the sauce base a little, add the juice, orange peel as well as the orange jam and cream, and let thicken again. Bind it with sauce thickener. Sprinkle in the remaining thyme leaves.

Brussels sprouts and iced chestnuts go well with this dish.

Pepper Sauce with Lamb Saddle

INGREDIENTS: 1¾ lbs lamb saddle without bones • salt • 3 teaspoons coarsely ground pepper • 2 tablespoons olive oil • 3½ oz cold butter • 4 stalks thyme • ½ cup sugar • 1 bundle young carrots • 2 kohlrabies • 12 small onions • 1 ⅔ cubs lamb broth • freshly ground pepper • 1 bunch chopped parsley

PREPARATION: Rub the meat with salt and coarsely ground pepper, heat oil, and roast the meat all over in it. Take the meat out of the pan and leave to cool. Grease a piece of aluminum foil with a little butter, put the meat, together with thyme stalks, on it, and wrap. Meanwhile, clean the vegetables, peel them, and cut in bite-sized pieces, then boil one after another in salty water until soft, rinse in ice-cold water,

and drain. Put the wrapped meat into boiling water, then set the pot aside, and let stand for about 8 minutes. Reduce the lamb broth to a half. Stir butter, cut in small pieces, with a blender into the sauce. Add the vegetables. Spice generously with salt and pepper and improve with parsley. Take the meat out of the foil and cut it diagonally into thin slices.

Roast potatoes with thyme, rosemary, and bay leaves go well with this dish.

Olive Thyme Butter with Lamb

INGREDIENTS: 12 simple lamb cutlets • 1 red chili pepper
• 1 stalk rosemary • 6 stalks thyme • 4 cloves of garlic •
8 tablespoons olive oil • ⅓ oz soft butter • ⅓ oz black
olives without pits • ½ teaspoon grated lemon peel of one
untreated fruit • 1 tablespoon chopped parsley • salt •
freshly ground pepper

PREPARATION: Wash the lamb cutlets and dry them. Cut chili
pepper, rosemary, and half of the thyme in small pieces.
Cut two garlic cloves into slices. Mix everything with olive
oil and spread the cutlets with it on both sides. Let sit for
12–24 hours. Meanwhile, whisk the butter until frothy. Cut
the olives in small cubes. Mix butter with olives, lemon
peel, parsley, the remaining chopped garlic and the
remaining thyme leaves, spice with salt and pepper. Form
a roll and wrap it in grease-proof paper and leave in a cool
place. Fry the lamb cutlets in a hot grill pan
on both sides for about 2 minutes. Cut the
butter in slices and serve on top of the lamb
cutlets.

As a side dish, ratatouille, fried zucchini, or mixed salad with a crispy baguette
are suitable.

Chicken Curry

INGREDIENTS: 1 chicken • fish sauce • 2 tablespoons yellow curry paste • 2 tablespoons palm sugar or brown sugar • 2 cups coconut milk • 1 pinch of saffron powder • 4 bay leaves • 1 chopped red chilli-pepper • 4 peeled garlic cloves garlic • 12 small, peeled white onions • 1 baby pineapple • 2 stalks of lemon grass • salt • cumin • 1 tablespoon red pepper grains

PREPARATION: Divide the chicken into 12 pieces, wash, and dry them. Put on a plate and drizzle with a bit of fish sauce. Meanwhile, stir the curry paste with palm sugar or brown sugar and ½ cup coconut milk at a mild heat until smooth. Add the remaining coconut milk, saffron, bay leaves, and chili. Halve the garlic and onions lenghtwise. Add them, together with the chicken pieces, to the coconut milk and cook at a mild heat for 10 minutes. Peel the pineapple and cut in small pieces. Cut the lower part of the lemon grass into fine slices. Add the pineapple and the lemon grass to the chicken and cook everything for about 25 minutes. Season the Curry with fish sauce, salt, cumin and red pepper grains.

Rice goes well with this.

Peanut Sauce for Saté Skewers

INGREDIENTS: 1 lb chicken breast fillet • 2 peeled onions • 3 peeled cloves of garlic • 1 teaspoon chopped ginger • 4–6 tablespoons sweet soy sauce • freshly ground pepper • peanut oil • dark sesame oil • 3 peeled shallots • 2 tablespoons soy oil • 1 cup peanut bullet • 1 tablespoon Samba Oleic (Chinese sharp spice paste) • 1 tablespoon soy sauce • 1 teaspoon sugar • salt • 2 tablespoons highly-concentrated vinegar • 1 red, chili pepper chopped • 1 lime in slices • wooden skewers

PREPARATION: Wash the meat and cut into cubes of about 1 inch size. Chop the onions and garlic finely. Put one half of garlic aside. Mix onions, garlic, ginger, and soy sauce. Spice generously with pepper and let the meat sit in it for 2–4 hours. Put 5 pieces of meat onto each skewer. Heat a little oil in a grilling pan and roast the skewers in it all over for about 8 minutes until they are golden brown. Drizzle with some drops of sesame oil. Dice the shallots very finely. Roast them with the remaining garlic in hot soy oil. Stir in 1 cup water, peanut butter, Samba Oleic, soy sauce, sugar, a bit of salt, and highly-concentrated vinegar until smooth. Let the sauce boil once. Sprinkle the Saté skewers with a bit of chili and serve with lime slices and the sauce.

Crispy rice crackers go well with this dish.

Mustard Sauce with Chicken Meatballs

INGREDIENTS: 1 lb chicken breast fillet • 1 bag of pre-packaged seasoning for roast ground meat • ½ cup double-cream fresh cheese • a bit of grated lemon peel • Mazola germ oil • 4 peeled shallots • ⅔ cup Chicken Bouillon • ⅔ cup cream • 3 tablespoons course ground mustard • lightly-colored sauce thickener • salt • freshly ground pepper • lemon juice

PREPARATION: Wash the meat, dry, and put it through a meat grinder. Mix it with meat seasoning, fresh cheese, and lemon peel. With wet hands form 8 balls out of the meat mixture. Heat a bit of germ oil in a pan and fry the balls in it all over until golden brown. For the sauce, dice the shallots finely and cook in fat until brown. Add broth and cream and let thicken a little. Stir in mustard it and, if desired, bind the sauce with a bit of sauce thickener. Season to taste with salt, pepper, and lemon juice.

Stewed kohlrabi slices and young carrots go well with this.

Leek Cream Sauce with Turkey Roulade

INGREDIENTS: 2 leeks • Fondor Sauce Base • 4 turkey schnitzels • 1 spice mixture • ½ cup double-cream fresh cheese • 2 tablespoons sunflower oil • 2 tablespoons white wine • ¾ cups cream • 1 packet Leek Cream Soup • freshly grated nutmeg

> **TIP**
> Instead of leek, the same amount of mushrooms and mushroom-cream soup can be used for the sauce.

PREPARATION: Cut only the lightly-colored part of the leek in thin strips. Wash the leek properly and boil in a little water with some of Fondor Sauce Base for 2 minutes. Let it drain in a strainer, saving 1½ cups of the stock. Wash the schnitzels and dry. Sprinkle them with the spice mixture and spread the fresh cheese on the top. Sprinkle with half of the leeks and roll up. Fix with wooden skewers or kitchen string. Preheat the oven to 400°F. Roast the roulades in hot oil for 5 minutes. Pour vegetable stock, white wine and cream over it. Stir in the leek cream soup and some of nutmeg. Bake roulades uncovered in the sauce for 20 minutes. Sprinkle with the remaining leek and cook for another 20 minutes.

New potatoes go well with this dish.

Chervil Mustard Sauce with Stuffed Turkey Breast

INGREDIENTS: 3 tablespoons pine nuts • 1 cup dried, diced apricots • 1 bundle chopped parsley • 4 tablespoons coarse mustard • 7 teaspoons highly-concentrated vinegar • 2 tablespoons breadcrumbs • 1 egg • 2 lbs turkey breast • 1 bundle cubed soup vegetables • 1 bundle thyme • 1 cup white wine • 1 teaspoon coarsely ground pepper • salt • 4 tablespoons butter • ¾ cups meat broth • ¾ cups cream • light sauce thickener • 1 bundle chopped chervil

PREPARATION: Roast pine nuts lightly, put some aside. Mix pine kernels with apricots, parsley, 2 tablespoons mustard, 1 teaspoon vinegar, breadcrumbs, and an egg. Cut a pocket in the meat, fill it and fix with a wooden skewer. Mix soup vegetables with coarsely chopped thyme, white wine, pepper and remaining vinegar. Marinate turkey breast in it for 3–5 hours. Dry meat and strain marinade. Salt and brown meat in butter. Pour broth and marinade over it. Cook for 60–70 minutes. Wrap meat in aluminum foil. Boil gravy with remaining mustard and cream and let it reduce a little. Bind with sauce thickener and stir in chervil. Slice meat and sprinkle with remaining chopped pine nuts. Young carrots, sugar husks, and potatoes go well with this dish.

Mushroom Red Wine Sauce with Turkey Cutlets

INGREDIENTS: 4 turkey cutlets • salt • freshly ground pepper • 4 slices bacon • 1 teaspoon tomato purée • 4 tablespoons chopped parsley • germ oil • 4 red peeled onions • 1 peeled clove of garlic • 4 tablespoons butter • 1½ small, brown champignons • 1 cup red wine • 1 double package of sauce for poultry

PREPARATION: Wash the meat and wipe dry. Spice with salt and pepper. Cover each piece with 1 bacon slice. Spread tomato purée on top and sprinkle with parsley. Fold the schnitzel up once and fix with a wooden skewer. Brown in hot oil on both sides. Cut the onions in thin strips. Chop garlic finely. Saute both in butter. Clean mushrooms and slice thinly. Add them to the onions and braise shortly. Add red wine and the same amount of water and boil for 5 minutes. Stir in sauce powder and let simmer for some minutes.

Savory potato salad goes well with this.

Coriander Plum Sauce with Marinated Duck Breast

INGREDIENTS: 2 peeled cloves of garlic • 7 tablespoons soy sauce • 7 tablespoons dry sherry • 7 tablespoons honey • 2 duck breast fillets • 2 tablespoons sunflower oil • 1 tablespoon peanut oil • 4 crushed coriander seeds • ground cloves • cinnamon • 3 tablespoons balm vinegar • 1 tablespoon lemon juice • 4–5 tablespoons plum purée • salt • freshly ground pepper • 4 golden, peeled kiwis

PREPARATION: Squeeze the garlic through a garlic press. Mix with soy sauce, sherry, and honey. Wash the meat, wipe it dry, and put with the marinade into a freezing bag. Let sit for 24 hours. Preheat the oven to 325 °F. Heat the oil, then salt and pepper the drained duck fillets. Roast the fillets on the skin side for 5 minutes, turn over, and put in the oven for 15–20 minutes. Cook the peanut oil with coriander shortly, stir in pinch of ground cloves and cinnamon, vinegar, lemon juice, and plum purée. Reduce until creamy. Cut meat and kiwis into slices.

Boiled potato dumplings go well with this dish.

Orange Sauce with Roast Duck

INGREDIENTS: 1 duck, about 4 lbs • salt • freshly ground pepper • 1 bundle thyme • 4 tablespoons butter • 3¼ cups duck broth • 4 red onions chopped • 1 bundle of soup vegetables in cubes • 3 untreated oranges • 6 Kumquats • dark sauce thickener • 2 tablespoons orange liquor

PREPARATION: Chop the duck into 8 to 12 parts, wash and wipe dry. Rub with salt and pepper. Strip bay leaves from their stems. Preheat the oven to 350°F. Brown duck in hot butter in a frying pan, then braise in the oven for 30 minutes. Add 1 cup hot water, thyme, half of the broth, onions, and soup vegetables and cook for another 30 minutes. Wash the oranges, wipe dry, and peel one of them with a zester. Squeeze two oranges out, peel the third carefully, and loosen the wedges. Halve and pit the Kumquats. Boil the orange peel in a bit of juice until soft. Add the orange juice with the remaining broth to the duck meat and cook for another 40–50 minutes. Wrap the duck parts in aluminum foil. Strain the sauce. Add Kumquats and boil down a little, bind it lightly with a sauce thickener. Season with salt and pepper. Add orange peel, wedges and liquor as well as the duck parts and heat once more.

Best served with wild rice and Brussels sprouts.

Calvados Apple Sauce with Guinea Fowl Breast

INGREDIENTS: 4 skinned guinea fowl breasts • 2 table-spoons melted butter • salt • freshly ground pepper • 1 teaspoon fresh rosemary • 2 tablespoons butter • 2 apples • 4 peeled onions • 1⅓ cup chicken broth • 3 tablespoons Calvados • 4 tablespoons whipped cream

PREPARATION: Wash the meat and wipe dry. Mix butter with salt, pepper, and rosemary and rub the meat with it. Heat the butter and brown the guinea fowl breasts on both sides in it for 1 minute. Take the meat out and wrap it in aluminum foil. Quarter the apples, peel, and core them. Cut one quarter into tiny cubes and dice the rest coarsely. Cut the onions into thin strips. Dice one half of an onion finely, add to the apple cubes and put aside. Braise onions and apples in the fat until soft. Add poultry broth and boil down to one third.

Purée with a hand blender, season with Calvados, salt and pepper. Add the meat, remaining onion and apple cubes and let simmer for 3 minutes. Arrange the meat onto preheated plates and stir cream into the sauce. Golden-yellow fried polenta or semolina circles are good side dishes.

Juniper Sauce with Grilled Quail

INGREDIENTS: 8 quails • ½ baguette • 7 oz marbled bacon • salt • freshly ground pepper • 2 stalks rosemary • 4 stalks parsley • ½ bundle fresh bay leaves • 2 tablespoons olive oil • 6 tablespoons butter • 1⅔ cups poultry broth • 3 ground juniper berries

PREPARATION: Wash the quails and wipe dry. Cut the baguette into 6 slices about ¾ inch thick. Remove gristle and skin from the bacon and cut it crosswise into finger thick slices. Preheat an oven to 375 °F. Season the quails inside and outside with salt and pepper. Fill the abdomens with rosemary and parsley. Put bacon, bay leaves, bread slices, and quails, one after another, onto a long, wooden skewer. Heat olive oil and 2 tablespoons butter in a pan and brown the quail skewers in it on all sides. Cook in the oven for about 20 minutes until ready. Keep pouring gravy, which makes itself, over the quails. Take the quails out of the oven and wrap them in aluminum foil. Pour chicken broth over the gravy, boil down a little and thicken with the remaining butter. Season to taste with salt, pepper and ground juniper berries. Broil the quails for 2 minutes and serve with the juniper sauce.

Artichoke Tomato Sauce with Rabbit

INGREDIENTS: 1 dressed rabbit • salt • freshly ground pepper • 4 artichokes • lemon juice • 1½ lb tomatoes • 2 peeled carrots • 1 stalk celery • 2 peeled onions • 4 tablespoons butter • 6 cloves garlic, crushed with the peel • 2 stalks thyme • 1 stalk rosemary

PREPARATION: Divide rabbit into 8 pieces, wash and wipe dry. Season with salt and pepper. Remove wooden and hard outer leaves from the artichokes. Pick the remaining leaves off the tops. Scoop out the inside – the "hay" – with a spoon or a cutter. Quarter the artichokes and put them immediately into cold lemon water. Remove the stems from the tomatoes and dice. Cut carrots and celery into about 2 in long pieces. Dice onions coarsely. Preheat the oven to 325°F. Grease a frying pan with soft butter and arrange rabbit, vegetables, onions, garlic and spice stalks in it. Cook in a preheated oven for about 1½ hours. Pour a little water over it from time to time. Turn the rabbit pieces occasionally and baste with the produced gravy. Wrap the meat in aluminum foil. Stir the gravy sauce well and warm the meat in it.

Wide noodles go well with this.

Mole with Turkey

INGREDIENTS: 1 turkey, about 8 lbs • salt • freshly ground pepper • 5 tablespoons soft butter • 1 chili chipotle • 3 chili anchos • 8 chili mulatos • 1 chili pasillas • 1 chopped onion • 5 chopped cloves of garlic • 4 oz lard • 4 chopped tomatoes • 1 small banana • 3½ tablespoons skinned almonds • 5 tablespoons peanuts • 3½ tablespoons pumpkin seeds • 5 tablespoons raisins • 5 tablespoons pitted prunes • 2 cups chicken broth • 1 tortilla • ½ hard roll • cumin • anise powder • cinnamon • allspice • ground coriander • 2 oz high-quality chocolate • sugar

PREPARATION: Rub the turkey with soft butter and sprinkle inside and outside with salt and pepper. Roast in the oven at 400 °F for 2 ½–3 hours. Turn often and baste with gravy. Soak chilies in lukewarm water for 50 minutes, cut open and pit. Cut them into small pieces. Cook onions and garlic in hot fat until brown, add tomatoes, banana, almonds, peanuts, pumpkin kernels, raisins, prunes, chilies and 1¼ cups broth to it and let simmer uncovered for 15 minutes. Fry tortilla well in a pan without fat. Dice the roll. Add both to the sauce, let boil up once, purée it, and strain. Season the Mole sauce to taste with 1 big pinch of spice powder and let the chocolate melt in it. Season with salt, pepper, and sugar. If desired, thin the sauce with the remaining broth.

Sauces for Fish & Seafood

Fish swim cheerfully in water so why shouldn't they also swim in a fine sauce in order to please our taste buds? Fish, particularly salt-water fish, is very healthy. Seafood tastes excellent and can be prepared quickly in a variety of ways. How would you like shrimp with butter sauce or a sorrel sauce for salmon? Do you remember the pickled, grilled herring of your youth? Here you will find the recipe. We have the most exquisite sauces for our most popular salt-water fish but also for pike, perch, tuna, sardines, sea bass, squid, mussels and, of course, our beloved shrimp.

Mango Mint Sauce with Cod Skewers

INGREDIENTS: 1¾ lbs cod fillets • bay leaves • 1 untreated lemon • 8 tablespoons olive oil • salt • freshly ground pepper • 6 stalks peppermint • 1 mango • ½ cup passion fruit juice • 1 teaspoon crushed red pepper

PREPARATION: Wash the fish and wipe dry. Dice into approximately 1 inch cubes and alternately put onto skewers with bay leaves. Wash lemon with hot water and rub dry. Peel with a zester. Squeeze out the juice. Mix half of the lemon juice with half of the cooking oil. Mix in salt and pepper. Brush the fish skewers with this mixture. Heat the remaining cooking oil in a frying pan, fry the skewers on

each side for approximately 10 minutes. Cut the peppermint leaves into narrow strips. Peel the mango, cut out the pit, heat the fruit with the nectar, then puree. Mix with mint, salt, pepper, lemon juice, peel, and crushed red pepper.

Curry rice tastes good with this.

Tomato Tarragon Sauce with Cod

INGREDIENTS: 1¾ lbs cod fillet • lemon juice • herb salt • freshly ground pepper • 3 tablespoons butter • 2 chopped shallots • 1 chopped clove of garlic • 2 tablespoons dill • ½ cup white wine • 2 bay leaves • 1 can pizza tomatoes • 2 tablespoons tomato paste • 2 peeled tomatoes with seeds removed • 4 tablespoons chopped tarragon • 2 tablespoons olive oil • 1¼ cup frozen peas.

PREPARATION: Wash the fish and wipe dry. Brush with lemon juice, salt, and pepper. Cut into 8 pieces. Melt 2 tablespoons butter in a pot, add the shallots, garlic, dill, wine and bay leaves and heat. Put the fish in the juice, cover and cook slowly for 8–10 minutes. Wrap the fish in aluminum foil. Strain the juice. Add the pizza tomatoes and tomato paste and cook until thick and creamy. Cut the tomatoes into narrow strips and add to the sauce. Season with herb salt, pepper, tarragon, and cooking oil. Cook the peas slowly in a little salt water and butter.

Tossed noodles in butter go well with this recipe.

Olive Oregano Sauce with Cod

TIP
These recipes can also be cooked on the grill. In this case, the aluminum foil is left open instead of closed as in the previous recipes.

INGREDIENTS: 1¾ lbs cod • lemon juice • garlic salt • salt • freshly ground pepper • 8 tablespoons olive oil • 4 tablespoons orange juice • 1 chopped clove of garlic • 4 tablespoons fresh oregano leaves • 4 tomatoes • 1 egg plant • 4 stalks thyme • 12 black, pitted olives.

PREPARATION: Wash the fish and wipe dry. Brush with lemon juice, salt, and pepper. Grease 4 sheets of aluminum foil with some cooking oil. Mix the remaining cooking oil with orange juice, oregano leaves, and garlic. Season with salt and pepper. Preheat the oven to 400°F. Wash the tomatoes and egg plant and remove the

stems. Cut both into slices and put onto the aluminum foil. Cut the olives into strips. Put the fish, thyme, and olives on top of the vegetables. Pour the seasoned oil over it and close the aluminum foil around it. Cook slowly in a preheated oven for 20–30 minutes.

Freshly baked Baguettes go well with this recipe.

Coriander Lemon Sauce with Fish Skewers

INGREDIENTS: 1¼ lbs ocean perch fillet • 1 lb plaice
• 2 tbsp sunflower oil • 2 tablespoons dried Sherry
• 3 tbsp fish sauce • 2 tbsp sweet soy sauce •
4 tablespoons salty soy sauce • 1 chopped clove of
garlic • 1 teaspoon coriander seeds • ½ teaspoon
turmeric • 1 red chili pepper chopped • juice and
peel of 1 lime • 2 chopped shallots • 2 tbsp butter •
1 cup fish stock • 1 tbsp light sauce-thickener • 8 oz
mascarpone cheese • juice and peel of 1 lemon •
salt • freshly ground pepper • sugar

> **TIP**
> All firm-skinned fish and
> shrimp can be used for fish
> skewers. Those who like it
> can also use precooked veg-
> etables like carrots, zucchi-
> ni, eggplants, onions, and
> raw tomatoes with the fish
> on the skewers.

PREPARATION: Wash and dry fish. Dice ocean perch
into 1 in cubes. Mix sunflower oil, sherry, fish
sauce, soy sauce, garlic, coriander, turmeric, chili, and
lime juice. Spread mixture onto the plaice fillets, roll up,
and cut once straight through middle. Put diced fish and
fish rolls alternately onto 4 skewers, place in baking dish
and add marinade. Let sit for 30 minutes. Preheat the oven
to 350°F. Bake 10–15 minutes. Brown shallots in hot butter, add fish stock and let thicken. Stir in mascarpone,
lemon juice and peel. Season to taste with salt, pepper
and sugar. Put fish onto plates and add hot sauce.

Robust Fish Casserole

INGREDIENTS: 1 lb cod • 3 tablespoons melted butter • 3 tablespoons oats • 1 cup boiled asparagus pieces • ½ cup asparagus pieces • ½ cup Greenland crabs • ½ cup mussel meat • 3 teaspoons instant oat flakes • ⅕ cup asparagus stock • ½ cup sour cream • salt • freshly ground pepper • 4 tablespoons chopped parsley • ½ cup grated Emmentaler cheese • tabs of butter

PREPARATION: Wash the fish and wipe dry. Grease a baking pan and sprinkle 1 teaspoon oats over it. Cut the fish into

bite-sized pieces. Put asparagus, crabs, and mussels into the baking pan. Preheat the oven to 400°F. Melt the remaining butter and stir in the instant flakes. Add the asparagus stock to the mix and add the sour cream to it and season to taste with salt, pepper, and parsley. Pour the sauce over the fish and sprinkle the remaining oats, cheese, and butter over the fish. Bake in a pre-heated oven for 15-20 minutes until golden.

This recipe goes well with cucumber salad and sour cream and a lot of chopped dill.

Tomato Paprika Sauce with Cod

INGREDIENTS: 4 cod steaks • 1 teaspoon lime juice • 1 cup tomatoes • 5 tablespoons Ajvar (ready-to-buy paprika purée) • 1 teaspoon soy sauce • 1 tablespoon tomato paste • Samba oleic • sugar • salt • freshly ground pepper • 2 tablespoons butter

PREPARATION: Rinse the cod. Wipe dry. Put onto a plate, drip lime juice over it and let cool for approximately 20 minutes in the refrigerator covered with aluminum foil. Skin the tomatoes, cut into quarters and core. Dice the tomato quarters and purée in a mixer with Ajvar, soy sauce and tomato paste. Season the purée to taste with samba oleic, sugar, salt, and pepper. Heat the butter in a large frying pan and put the cod filets into it. Cover and let the fish steam slowly. Turn them once. Shortly before the end of cooking let them cook for approximately 2 minutes uncovered. Salt and pepper the cod and serve with cold tomato paste. Firm, white bread with garlic butter goes well with this meal.

TIP
Hot and cold united. A cold, hearty sauce of tomatoes and Ajvar – store-bought paprika purée – to go with the hot fish.

Pickled Grilled Herring

INGREDIENTS: 2 lbs pre-cooked herring • 6 tablespoons flour • salt • freshly ground pepper • sunflower oil • ½ cup red, peeled onions • 1½ oz grated ginger • 2 red chili peppers in rings • 1 cup hard cider • 5 tablespoons highly-concentrated vinegar • 10 crushed juniper berries • 3 teaspoons coriander seeds • 1–2 tablespoons brown sugar

PREPARATION: Wash the fish and wipe dry. Mix the flour with salt and plenty of pepper. Roll the fish in the mixture. Brown on both sides in hot cooking oil. Drain fat on paper towels. Then place in a wide baking dish. Cut the onions into rings. Boil with ginger, chili, hard cider, highly concentrated vinegar, 1 cup water, juniper berries, coriander, salt, and some sugar for 3 minutes. Season with salt, pepper, and sugar and pour lightly-cooled onto the herrings. Let chill for 1–2 days uncovered. Crispy fried potatoes and lettuce go well with this recipe.

Marinated Halibut

INGREDIENTS: 4 halibut steaks • salt • freshly ground pepper • 2 untreated lemons • 1 peeled clove of garlic • 1 bunch chopped parsley • 6 tablespoons olive oil • 6 tablespoons butter • 5 peeled shallots • 2 tablespoons small capers

PREPARATION: Wash the fish and wipe dry. Rub with salt and pepper. Wash the lemons with hot water and dab dry. Peel one lemon with a zester. Squeeze out juice and cut the other lemon into thin slices. Squeeze out the garlic through a pressing tool. Mix with the lemon juice, lemon peel, parsley, and 3 tablespoons cooking oil. Spread it onto the fish and put the fish into baking dish. Melt butter and briefly brown the shallots in it. Add the remaining oil and capers. Put the slices of lemon on the fish cutlets and pour the shallots with the fat over the cutlets. Let sit and cool for 2 hours in the refrigerator without a cover. Preheat the oven to 400°F. Cook the fish slowly for 20–25 minutes in the preheated oven.

Italian white bread and tomato salad with some garlic and Rugola go well with this recipe.

Creamy Cheese Sauce with Salmon

INGREDIENTS: 1¾ lbs salmon fillets • lemon juice • salt • freshly ground pepper • 1 lb beef tomatoes • 2 peeled onions • 2 peeled garlic cloves • 4 tablespoons butter • 4 tablespoons chopped parsley • 1 teaspoon fresh thyme • 1 teaspoon fresh marjoram • butter • 2 oz breadcrumbs • 3½ oz grated Pecorino cheese • ½ cup Crème Fraiche • ¾ cup cream

PREPARATION: Wash the fish, wipe dry, and cut into large pieces. Pour lemon juice on the pieces and sprinkle it with salt and pepper. Wash the tomatoes and remove the stems. Cut into thick slices. Cut the onions into rings. Chop the garlic finely. Preheat the oven to 400°F. Butter a baking dish well. Put the tomato slices, onions, garlic, and herbs into the pan. Sprinkle with salt and pepper. Put the fish on top of the ingredients. Mix the breadcrumbs with half of the cheese, salt, and pepper. Spread this mixture on the

pieces of fish. Warm the remaining cheese with Crème Fraiche and cream. Season it with salt and pepper. Pour the sauce over the fish and bake until brown in a preheated oven for 15–20 minutes.

Goes well with big bowl of mixed salad with herb dressing.

Green Asparagus Sauce with Salmon

INGREDIENTS: ¾ lb green asparagus • 2 cups vegetable stock • 1 cup cream • 2 tablespoons double cream • ⅓ cup dry white wine • salt • freshly ground pepper • lemon juice • 4 7 oz salmon fillets

PREPARATION: Peel only the bottom part of the asparagus. Cut away the heads. Cook in the hot vegetable stock for 4 minutes, take them out, and drain. Cut the remaining asparagus stalks into small pieces and boil them until soft in the vegetable stock. Take the asparagus pieces out and puree. Thicken the cream somewhat with the double cream and white wine. Add the asparagus puree to the mix and season to taste with salt, pepper, and lemon juice. Add the asparagus heads to the sauce. Wash the fish and let it cook in the hot vegetable stock at mild heat for 5–8 minutes. Put the salmon fillets into the asparagus sauce and serve.

Fresh potatoes with parsley and butter go well with this recipe.

Sorrel with Salmon

INGREDIENTS: 4 salmon steaks • some butter • 2 table-spoons lemon juice • 2 tablespoons olive oil • salt • fresh-ly ground pepper • 2 oz sorrel • 1 pouch of refined Crème Fraiche sauce • 2 tablespoons white wine

PREPARATION: Preheat the oven to 400°F. Cut the middle bone out of the steaks, wash the fish and wipe dry. Butter a baking dish and put the salmon steaks next to each other in it. Mix the lemon juice with 1 tablespoon water, cooking oil, salt, and pepper. Pour the mixture over the fish.

Cook the fish slowly in a preheated oven 5–6 minutes. Wash the sorrel and pick off the leaves from the stems. Chop the leaves coarsely. Stir the Crème Fraiche into 1 cup luke-warm water and bring to a boil while stirring. Add the sorrel, wine, and cooked fish juice to the sauce and puree.

Young potatoes taste good with this recipe.

Horseradish Sauce with Salmon

INGREDIENTS: 1 ¾ lb salmon steaks • 4 teaspoons highly-concentrated vinegar • 1 bundle of dill • 4 triangular Yufka leaves • salt • freshly ground pepper • 1 cup peanut oil • ¾ cup cream • 1 tablespoon sugar • 5–6 tablespoons grated horseradish • 1 lime

> **TIP**
> You can find Yufka leaves in Turkish grocery stores.

PREPARATION: Wash the fish and wipe dry. Cut into four parts. Mix 1 teaspoon concentrated vinegar with 3 teaspoons water and spread on salmon. Wash the dill, spin dry and remove the stems. Chop half coarsely and put aside. Put the Yufka leaves next to each other on paper towels and moisten with water. Place the fillets on them widthwise and sprinkle with salt and pepper and dill. Carefully wrap the fish in the dough and fry in hot cooking oil for 8–10 minutes. Use paper towels to absorb the extra fat. Whip the cream with sugar until semi-stiff. Fold in the remaining vinegar, horseradish, and chopped dill. Season with salt and pepper. Cut the lime into slices and serve with the fish and horseradish sauce.

Good with peeled tomatoes tossed in butter and broccoli.

Cress Sauce with Smoked Trout and Asparagus

INGREDIENTS: 3 lbs asparagus • salt • 1 teaspoon sugar • 1 teaspoon butter • 1 lemon peel • 1 stalk parsley • ½ cup full-fat cream cheese • 3 tablespoons Crème Fraiche • 1 teaspoon mustard • 2 tablespoons lemon juice • 1 teaspoon honey • freshly ground pepper • 2 bunches cress • ½ cup whipped cream • 4 smoked trout fillets • 4 large radishes

PREPARATION: Peel the asparagus carefully and cut the stringy parts away. Bring approximately 1 liter water with salt, sugar, butter, lemon peel, and parsley to a boil. Let the asparagus cook in the water slowly for 10 minutes. Drain and let cool. Stir in the cream cheese with Crème Fraiche, mustard, lemon juice, honey, salt, and pepper. Add the small leaves from one and a half beets to the cream cheese mixture and stir the cream. Divide the asparagus onto plates and add the trout and the sauce to it.

Buttered and toasted bread goes well with this recipe.

Tomato Sugo with Salmon Carpaccio

INGREDIENTS: 1 red pepper, chopped chili • 1 table-spoon chopped, fresh ginger • 2 chopped cloves of garlic • 1 chopped shallot • ⅔ lb tomatoes • 3½ oz yellow paprika • 2 tablespoons olive oil • 3 tea-spoons highly-concentrated vinegar • 5 tablespoons vegetable stock • salt • freshly ground pepper • 1 teaspoon honey • 1 bundle of rugola • ½ lb thinly sliced salmon

> **TIP**
> For this fine little dish you can use fresh salmon as well as slices of smoked salmon or graved lax.

PREPARATION: Mix chili with ginger, garlic and the shal-lot. Blanch, skin, core and cube tomatoes. Peel the paprika with a peeling tool and cut into fine cubes, then put them to the side. Heat the cooking oil and fry the chili-shallot mix for a short time. Add tomatoes, vinegar and vegetable stock and let boil for a short time. Season generously with salt, pepper and honey. Stir in the papri-ka cubes and let cool. Wash the rugola and spin dry. Chop half of the leaves coarsely and mix with the tomato juice. Serve the salmon with the sugo and garnish with the remaining rugola leaves. Good with whole grain bread with chives or garlic butter.

Herb Hollandaise with Smoked Salmon Omelet

INGREDIENTS: 2 lbs white asparagus • salt • 1 pinch sugar • 1 teaspoon butter • 1 shallot • 5 white peppercorns • 1 tablespoon white wine vinegar • 3 egg yolks • 1 cup butter • freshly ground pepper • 1 tablespoon lemon juice • 2 tablespoons chopped parsley • 2 tablespoons chopped dill • 8 eggs • 4 tablespoons cream • freshly grated nutmeg • 3 tablespoons butter • 10 oz smoked salmon slices

PREPARATION: Peel the asparagus and remove the stringy ends. Cook in boiling salt water with sugar and butter slowly for 12 minutes. Peel the shallot, cube finely and reduce by simmering lightly with the grated peppercorns, vinegar and five tablespoons of water for 5 minutes. Strain into a steel bowl. Whisk the egg yolks in a double boiler. Whisk in the

shallot-egg-mixture until creamy. Take the bowl out of the double boiler, carefully add melted, but-not-too-hot butter while stirring-constantly. Season with salt, pepper and lemon juice. Stir in chopped herbs. Whisk cream and eggs and season with salt, pepper, and nutmeg. Deep-fry 4 omelets in butter. Drain asparagus. Fill the omelets with asparagus, salmon and herb-hollandaise

Caper Tomato Sauce for Pike

INGREDIENTS: 1¾ lbs tomatoes • 1 peeled clove of garlic • 2 peeled onions • 2 tablespoons butter • 1 bay leaf • some grated lemon peel • 2 stalks thyme • 2 tablespoons tomato paste • salt • sugar • freshly ground pepper • 2–3 tablespoons small capers • 4 pike with skin à 5 oz each • 6 tablespoons olive oil • 4 tablespoons lime juice • 1 bundle of chopped parsley

PREPARATION: Blanch the tomatoes in boiling water for a short time. Remove the stems, skin, core and dice. Let the garlic and onions fry until light brown in hot butter. Add diced tomatoes, bay leaf, lemon peel, thyme and tomato paste and cook until thick and creamy. Season the sauce to taste with salt, sugar, pepper, and capers. Wash the fish and wipe dry. Brush with salt and pepper and fry in hot cooking oil on both sides for a total of 4–5 minutes until golden yellow. Stir in the lime juice and parsley into the cooking fat and pour over the fish. Serve with the sauce.

Fried potatoes, rice, or crispy white bread go well with this recipe.

TIP
This spicy, light, sour sauce also tastes good with cod, shellfish, ocean perch or coalfish.

Monkfish and Tomato Skewers

INGREDIENTS: 1¾ lbs monkfish • 10 cherry tomatoes •
1 garlic clove • 2 tablespoons lemon juice • ½ cup white
wine • 2 bay leaves • 2 stalks rosemary • 4 tablespoons
cooking oil • freshly ground pepper

PREPARATION: Wash the fish and wipe dry. Cut the monkfish
into approximately 1½ inch pieces. Wash and halve the cherry tomatoes. Put the fish and tomatoes in a flat dish. Peel

the garlic and squeeze through a garlic
press. Add the garlic to the lemon juice,
white wine, bay leaves, and rosemary and
bring everything to a boil. Let the marinade
cool, and then pour it over the fish and the
tomatoes. Let stand uncovered for 2 hours.
Drain the fish and tomatoes well, alternately place them on skewers and brush with
cooking oil. Put aluminum foil on the grill
rack and grill the skewers on it at medium
heat for approximately 7 minutes. Halfway
through the cooking time, turn the skewers
over. You can also fry the skewers in
a grilling pan. Season with freshly ground
pepper.

Spaghetti with the finest olive oil, some lemon juice and
pressed garlic go well with this recipe.

Fennel Orange Sauce with Monkfish

INGREDIENTS: 3 untreated blood oranges • 10½ oz fennel • 4 tablespoons butter • 1 teaspoon fennel seeds • ½ cup Crème double • 1 green chili pepper • salt • freshly ground pepper • 2 lb monkfish • 1 lb peeled onions • 4 peeled garlic cloves • 1 untreated lemon • 2 bay leaves • ½ cup olive oil

TIP
Spicy Ciabatta bread is best with this recipe.

PREPARATION: Wash oranges and wipe dry. Peel 2 fruits with a zester, squeeze out the fruit, and peel the third fruit and slices it. Clean the fennel, cut into narrow strips, and put the tender greens to the side. Melt the butter, then add orange juice, fennel, and fennel seeds and cook until soft. Stir in the double cream and puree. Mince the chili pepper. Add half of the orange peel, orange filets, and chili to the sauce and season to taste with salt and pepper. Sprinkle with the torm fennel greens. Cut the monkfish into slices. Preheat the oven to 400°F. Spread the sliced onions and garlic on the bottom of a roasting pan. Season the monkfish with salt and pepper and put it on top of the onions. Wash the lemon in hot water, wipe dry and cut it into thin slices. Put the lemon and bay leaves on top of the monkfish. Pour olive oil over it and let cook slowly without a cover in a preheated oven for 30–40 minutes. Pour the sauce on a dish, add the monkfish and replace the bay leaves with the remaining orange peels.

Olive Caper Sauce with Swordfish

INGREDIENTS: 2 1 lb swordfish steaks • salt • freshly ground pepper • 2 peeled garlic cloves • 6 oz black olives without pits • 4 tablespoons capers • 4 tablespoons olive oil • 4 tablespoons cold butter • some lemon juice • 4 table-spoons chopped parsley

PREPARATION: Wash the fish and wipe dry. Season with salt and pepper and fry on each side in a lightly oiled pan

for 6 minutes. Meanwhile, cut the garlic cloves into thin slices and halve the olives. Chop the capers coarsely. Drizzle olive oil onto the swordfish and take out of the frying pan after cooking an additional 3 minutes. Place on a preheated plate. Add butter to pan, then flavor with olives, capers and lemon juice. Season with salt and pepper. Garnish with parsley and pour the sauce over the swordfish.

Good with fresh white bread or olive bread.

Lemon Sauce with Sea Bass

INGREDIENTS: 1¾ lbs whole sea bass • salt • freshly ground pepper • ½ bunch smooth parsley • 2 stalks thyme • 2 bay leaves • flour for dusting • 2 tablespoons olive oil • 3 tablespoons capers • 2 lemons • 6 tablespoons butter

PREPARATION: Wash the fish and wipe dry. Cut three to 4 parallel slits behind the head on both sides with a sharp knife so that the fish can cook evenly. Season the sea bass on the inside and outside with salt and pepper and fill the belly with some parsley stalks, 1 stalk thyme and one bay leaf. Dust the skin lightly with flour. Preheat the oven to 350°F. Heat the olive oil in a large frying pan and let the fish fry in it on both sides. After 3 minutes turn the fish over. In the frying pan, cook slowly in a preheated oven for approximately 12 minutes until finished, constantly basting with pan juices. Chop the capers coarsely. Peel the lemons with a knife so that the zest is completely removed. Slice the lemons with a sharp knife. Pluck the leaves from the remaining parsley stalks and chop coarsely. Take the fish out of the oven and pour off the oil. Let butter froth up in a frying pan and add the capers, lemon filets, remaining thyme, 1 bay leaf, and the parsley. Season with salt and pepper. Place the sea bass on a plate and pour the lemon sauce on it. White bread or rice goes well with this recipe.

Egg Tomato Sauce with Sardines

INGREDIENTS: 24 fresh sardines • 1 Radicchio • flour for dusting • 10 tablespoons olive oil • salt • freshly ground pepper • 3 tomatoes • 2 hard-boiled eggs • 3 tablespoons balsamic vinegar • 6 tablespoons olive oil • 1 pinch sugar • several basil leaves

PREPARATION: Cut open the belly of the sardines and carefully remove the head with the fish bones. Rinse the sardines well under cold flowing water and wipe dry. Pull out the stalk from the Radicchio and cut the head into 1 centimeter wide slices. Put on a large plate. Roll the sardines in flour on both sides and fry golden brown in hot cooking oil. Salt and pepper, then take them out of the frying pan and degrease on kitchen paper towels. Remove the stems from the tomatoes and put into boiling water. Skin the fruits, quarter, core and dice finely. Peel the eggs and chop finely. Add the chopped eggs to the balsamic vinegar and olive oil. Add the tomatoes and season with salt, sugar, and pepper. Heat the sauce. Put the sardines onto the salad and pour the egg tomato sauce over it. Garnish with fresh basil.

Spicy white bread with garlic or tomato butter goes well with this recipe.

Saffron Cilantro Sauce for Tuna

INGREDIENTS: ½ cup vegetable stock • 1 small can of saffron powder • 1 pouch instant Hollandaise sauce • 4 oz cold butter • 4 tablespoons chopped cilantro • 1 lime • 4 5 oz tuna steaks • one packet of mixed seasoning • 2 tablespoons sunflower oil

> **TIP**
> Never let tuna fillets fry too long because they will dry out. Pay attention to the freshness quality when you buy the fish.

PREPARATION: Mix the vegetable stock with saffron powder and stir in the powdered sauce with a whisk. Bring to a boil. Stir the butter into the sauce in little flakes. Stir in the cilantro and do not let the sauce boil any longer. Wash the lime with hot water and dab dry. Grate part of the peel into the sauce. Squeeze out the fruit and season the sauce to taste with some lime juice. Wash the fish and wipe dry. Brush with the mixed seasoning and let the fish fry for one minute in hot oil on each side. Drizzle with lime juice and pour the sauce over the fish.

Whole grain rice with roasted cashews goes well with this recipe.

Shrimp Butter Sauce with Salmon Steaks

PREPARATION: 4 salmon steaks • some lime juice • salt • freshly ground pepper • 2 tablespoons cooking fat • 1 lb shrimp with heads • 6 tablespoons butter • 2 chopped shallots • 1 chopped clove of garlic • 1 cup white wine • 3 tablespoons white port wine • 1 bay leaf • 1 tablespoon flour • ¾ cup cream • some dill

PREPARATION: Wash the fish and wipe dry. Brush with lime juice and season with salt and pepper. Fry the steaks in hot cooking fat on each side for 3–4 minutes. Shell the shrimp and remove the heads and skin. Fry the shrimp shells in one tablespoon hot butter until brown. Add the shallots, garlic clove, white wine, port wine, and bay leaf and simmer uncovered for 10 minutes. Strain the juice. Melt 3 tablespoons butter and fry the flour in it until brown. Pour in the shrimp juice and cream and simmer for 10 minutes. Season to taste with salt, pepper, and lime juice. Add the shrimp, remaining butter, and some dill and heat it up. Pour the sauce over the salmon steaks.

Fresh potatoes or long-grained rice go well with this recipe.

White Wine Tomato Sauce with Mussels

PREPARATION: 3 cloves of garlic • 5 spring onions • ¼ celery root • 1 carrot • 5 tablespoons olive oil • 1 stalk rosemary • ½ teaspoon dried thyme • 1 large can tomatoes • 4 lbs mussels • 2 cups dry white wine • salt • freshly ground pepper • cayenne pepper

> **TIP**
> Opened mussels before preparation and closed mussels after preparation must be thrown away as they are spoiled.

PREPARATION: Peel the garlic and cut it into thin slices. Skin the spring onion and cut it into narrow strips along with the onion greens. Peel the celery and carrot. Cut the celery into small cubes and cut the carrot into slices. Heat cooking oil in a very large pot or in a casserole dish. Add prepared vegetables and let steam for a short time. Stir the herbs and tomatoes into the juice and let simmer softly for approximately 15 minutes. Clean the mussels very well under flowing water with a brush. Add wine to the tomato sauce and bring to a boil. Remove the rosemary and season the sauce according to taste with salt, pepper, and cayenne pepper. Add the mussels to the tomato sauce and let them cook slowly at high heat in a closed pot. Shake the pot well now and then. Distribute the mussels and sauce onto preheated bowls after approximately 10 minutes of cooking.

Oven fresh baguettes are good for sopping up this sauce.

Tomato Cream with Squid Rings

TIP

You can find squid rings in well-stocked fish stores or in the deep-freezer section of a good supermarket.

INGREDIENTS: 1¾ lbs frozen squid rings • juice from 1 lemon • ½ bundle of chervil • 5 beef tomatoes • ½ cup white wine • 4 tablespoons olive oil • 4 chopped garlic cloves • salt • lemon pepper • ½ cup Crème Fraiche

PREPARATION: Thaw the squid and wipe dry. Drizzle lemon juice on the squid. Chop the chervil. Blanch tomatoes in boiling water for a short time, skin, quarter, and core them. Cut the tomatoes into fine cubes and pour along with white wine in a mixer. Purée on the highest level. Heat the cooking oil in a frying pan, fry the squid rings, add garlic and season to taste with salt and pepper. Take the squid out of the frying pan. Add the tomato puree and Crème Fraiche to the frying pan, let cook well and season to taste with salt and pepper. Serve the squid with the tomato cream and chervil.

Mussel Sauce with Stuffed Calamari

INGREDIENTS: 4 4 oz squid tentacles • 2 oz raisins • 1 cup black tea • 1½ oz pine nuts • 1 tomato • ½ cup Ricotta • 2 egg yolks • 2½ oz grated white bread • ½ bunch chopped parsley • salt • freshly ground pepper • 2 tablespoons olive oil • 2 red peppers, quartered • 3 oz boned mussel meat • 2 stalks oregano

PREPARATION: Wash the squid and wipe dry from the inside out. Let the raisins soak in tea. Roast the pine nuts lightly in a frying pan without fat and chop coarsely. Remove the tomato stems and cut a cross in the skin. Put the tomatoes into boiling water and skin, quarter, core and dice into small pieces. Mix the Ricotta, egg yolks, grated white bread, some parsley, pine nuts and the drained raisins and season with salt and pepper. Stuff tentacles with mixture, secure ends with toothpicks and season with salt and pepper. Preheat the oven to 350°F. Cook the squid in hot olive oil on all sides until brown. Quarter the peppers, add to squid and cook slowly approximately 30 minutes, constantly basting with water. Add the mussels shortly before the end of the cooking time and heat it up with the cooking juice. Serve the squid on the peppers and pour the mussel sauce onto it. Sprinkle with fresh oregano leaves.

Good with crispy baguettes.

Orange Sauce with Shrimp Asparagus Ragout

INGREDIENTS: 3 lbs asparagus • 1 cup sugar peas • 16 large, raw shrimp without head or shells • salt • sugar • 1 tablespoon butter • 1 onion • 3½ tablespoons crab butter • 2¼ cups lobster juice • ½ cup cream • ⅛ cup vermouth • 4 tablespoons orange juice • peel from 1 organic orange • 3 tablespoons sauce thickener • freshly ground pepper • 1 tablespoon chopped dill

PREPARATION: Peel the asparagus and remove the stringy ends. Wash the sugar peas, clean, and cut into pieces. Wash the shrimp, wipe dry, and remove the entrails. Cut asparagus into small pieces and cook slowly in boiling salt water with some sugar and butter for 10 minutes. Add sugar peas and cook for an additional 5 minutes. Peel the onions, dice and steam in 1½ tablespoons crab butter. Pour in the lobster juice and let simmer for 10 minutes. Add the cream, vermouth, orange juice, and orange peel. Boil. Stir in the sauce thickener and season with salt, pepper and dill. Cook the shrimp in the remaining crab butter for 3 minutes, halve, and add to the sauce. Drain asparagus and sugar peas and pour the shrimp ragout over them. Good with aromatic Basmati rice, chopped pistachios and brown butter.

> **TIP**
> Never cook the shrimp too long because they will become hard very quickly. A few minutes, according to the amount being cooked, is sufficient.

Garlic Herb Butter with Shrimp

INGREDIENTS: 24 shrimp with heads and shells • 2 cloves of garlic • ½ cup butter • ½ bunch chives • 4 tablespoons chopped parsley • 4 tablespoons chopped dill • salt • freshly ground pepper • ½ teaspoon grated lemon peel

> **TIP**
>
> Shrimp tastes best cooked in the shell since the shell lends its taste to the meat. Shrimp or freshwater crayfish are also served in the best restaurants without silverware. Lemon water can be provided for rinsing the fingers.

PREPARATION: Wash the shrimp and dry. Preheat the oven to 375°F. Grease a baking dish with some butter. Season the shrimp with salt and pepper and put it into the baking dish. Bake slowly for approximately 10 minutes. Meanwhile, cut the washed chives finely. Peel the garlic cloves and squeeze through a pressing tool. Stir the remaining butter until frothy and mix with garlic, parsley, chives, and dill. Season with salt, pepper, and grated lemon peel. Take the shrimp out of the oven and cover with herb butter. Cook for an additional 5 minutes on high heat in the oven.

Tuscan white bread goes well with this recipe.

Paprika Tomato Sauce with Jumbo Shrimp Skewers

TIP
Shrimp skewers can easily be prepared on the grill. Spread olive oil or melted garlic butter on them.

INGREDIENTS: 1⅔ lbs tomatoes • 1 red pepper • 4 tablespoons olive oil • 1 teaspoon of dried Italian herbs • 1 chopped garlic clove • salt • 1 pinch of sugar • 1 lemon pepper • 24 jumbo shrimp without heads or shells • 4 tablespoons of cooking fat

PREPARATION: Dip the tomatoes in boiling water, skin, quarter and core. Cut the tomatoes and pepper into small cubes. Heat the olive oil in a pot. Cook the tomatoes and red pepper while stirring until they are creamy and thick. Season to taste with herbs, garlic, salt, sugar and pepper. Place 6 shrimps at a time onto a skewer. Heat the cooking fat in a large frying pan. Fry the skewers on both sides, approximately 5 minutes, over medium heat. Serve the sauce to the side.

Vegetable salad made of cauliflower and broccoli in a light sauce made of yogurt, tomato ketchup, mayonnaise, and brandy go well with this recipe.

Asian Marinade for Shrimp

INGREDIENTS: 1 lb shrimp without heads or shells • 2 garlic cloves • 1 stalk lemon grass • 1 tablespoon freshly grated ginger • 1 teaspoon turmeric • 2 tablespoons lemon juice • 4 tablespoons of peanut oil • 4 tablespoons soy sauce • 1 tablespoon fish sauce • 10 basil leaves

PREPARATION: Wash the shrimp and remove the entrails. Peel the garlic cloves and chop finely. Halve the lemon grass lengthwise, remove the outermost leaves, and cut the inner white part into fine strips. For the marinade, stir the garlic, lemon grass, ginger, and turmeric with lemon juice, cooking oil, soy sauce, and fish sauce. Mix the shrimp with the marinade and let stand covered for approximately 2 hours. Put the shrimp onto oiled skewers and grill at high heat for 5–6 minutes until transparent. Turn the skewers multiple times. Wash the basil leaves, spin dry, chop finely, and sprinkle over the hot shrimp.

Saffron-yellow long-grain rice goes well with the colorful pepper slices.

TIP
Shrimp of every size are available fresh as well as frozen. Even when the shrimp is fresh, in most cases, it has been thawed.

Sauces for Vegetables

People should consume a large amount of vegetables every day. They taste good and are healthy. However, adding only butter to the vegetables becomes boring after a while. In this chapter you will find a series of fine sauce for vegetable dishes. What do you think of wild herb sauces with bear leek and nettle? Try the colorful, tasty and exceptional horseradish red beet sauce for black salsify. We serve a green Béchamel sauce for fruity green tomatoes and prepare fennel and tomato in a coconut curry sauce. Have you ever tried a tomato sauce with peppermint or a creamy Gorgonzola sauce for a juicy Zucchini Flan? The result are two simple, but sophisticated egg dishes.

Bear Leek Sauce with Potato Casserole

TIP
Bear leek is available in spring at the weekend farmer's market.

INGREDIENTS: 1 lb boiling potatoes • 4 eggs • salt • freshly ground pepper • freshly ground nutmeg • 7 oz aged Gouda Cheese • 4 tablespoons butter • 4 chopped shallots • 1 package Hollandaise sauce • lemon juice • 1 cup of chopped bear leek leaves • ½ cup whipped cream

PREPARATION: Cook the potatoes slowly in a little water for 25 minutes. Peel the potatoes and put them through a press. Separate the eggs. Whip the egg whites with some salt until stiff. Add the egg yolks with salt, pepper, and nutmeg to the potatoes and mix well. Cut the cheese into little cubes. Add 3 tablespoons butter to the potato mix and stir in the cheese. Fold in the beaten egg whites. Preheat the oven to 400°F. Grease a baking dish with butter and put the potatoes in it. Cover with a few pats of butter and cook until golden brown in the oven for 20–30 minutes. Melt the remaining butter and fry the shallots in it until brown. Add the sauce and bring to a boil. Season to taste with nutmeg, lemon juice, and pepper. Stir in bear leeks and fold in whipped cream.

Nettle Sauce with Asparagus and Tofu Balls

INGREDIENTS: 3 lbs asparagus • salt • sugar • 1 teaspoon instant vegetable stock • 2 chopped shallots • 1 chopped garlic clove • 4 tablespoons butter • 1 teaspoon fresh grated ginger • cumin • 1 egg • 2–3 tablespoons breadcrumbs • 1¼ cups of tofu • 1 tablespoon flour • ¾ cup cream • ¾ cups sour cream • 6 tablespoons young chopped nettle leaves • lemon juice • 2 tablespoons chopped parsley

PREPARATION: Peel the asparagus and cut away the stringy ends. Cook slowly in boiling salt water with some sugar for 12 minutes. Drain and keep warm. Reduce stock to approximately 3 cups and add broth. Cook shallots and garlic in 2 tablespoons of butter, ginger and some cumin until brown. Stir in the salt and pepper and let cool. Add the egg, breadcrumbs and the crushed tofu and stir well. Melt the remaining butter in a pan, add the flour and ½ cup broth. Let the sauce simmer for 5 minutes. Form small balls out of the tofu mix and let cook slowly for 10 minutes in boiling water. Add the cream and sour cream to the sauce and heat. Stir in the nettles and lemon juice. Prepare the tofu balls and asparagus, top with the sauce and sprinkle with parsley.

Good with curry rice.

Green Asparagus in Orange Lemon Marinade

INGREDIENTS: 2 lbs green asparagus • salt • sugar • 1 tea-spoon butter • juice and peel from one untreated lemon • juice and peel from one untreated orange • freshly ground pepper • 4 tablespoons sunflower oil • 1 bunch chives • lemon balm

PREPARATION: Wash the asparagus and peel the lower part, removing the stringy ends. Cook in boiling salt water with some sugar and butter. Drain and put in a flat dish. Wash the lemon and orange with hot water, rub dry, and grate

the peels to half their thickness and squeeze out the juice. Mix the lemon and orange juices with salt, pepper, and oil into a marinade. Wash the chives, dry, chop finely, and add to the marinade. Pour the marinade over the asparagus, sprinkle with lemon peel, and let sit for 2 hours. Before serving, garnish with lemon balm.

Toasted and buttered bread goes well with this recipe.

Chervil Sauce with Asparagus

INGREDIENTS: 1¾ lbs green asparagus • 1¾ lbs white asparagus • salt • sugar • 4 tablespoons butter • 5 tablespoons pumpkin seeds • 1 teaspoon pumpkin seed oil • ½ cup Crème Fraiche • 1 blood orange • freshly ground pepper • cayenne pepper • 6 tablespoons chopped chervil

PREPARATION: Peel the green asparagus only on the bottom part and completely peel the white asparagus. Put the white asparagus into boiling salt water with some sugar and some butter and cook slowly for 5 minutes. Add the green asparagus and cook slowly for an additional 7 minutes. Roast the pumpkin seeds in a frying pan without fat, then mix with oil and puree with Crème Fraiche. Squeeze out the orange and add to the Crème Fraiche. Season to taste with salt, pepper, and cayenne pepper. Stir in the chervil.

> **TIP**
> Asparagus does not always have to be served hot. The subtle taste of asparagus is outstandingly suitable for all sorts of spices and herbs. Marinated asparagus as an impressive appetizer is particularly popular.

Small, diced, crispy fried potato cubes go well with this recipe.

Horseradish Red Beet Sauce with Black Salsify

INGREDIENTS: 2 lbs black salsify • juice from one lemon • salt • 1 teaspoon vegetable stock granules • freshly ground pepper • ½ lb red beets • 3½ tablespoons fresh horseradish • 1 cup sour cream • Worcestershire sauce • sugar

TIP

The red beet has a very intense color. Therefore, if you do not want red hands, you should wear gloves while working with this bulb.

PREPARATION: Brush off the black salsify under running water, peel, and immediately put in a bowl with lemon juice so that it does not become discolored. Put the black salsify in a pot, cover with water, some lemon juice, broth granules, salt, and pepper. Boil for 12–15 minutes slowly, then strain and reserve some of the stock. Keep warm. Wash the red beet and boil until soft in a lot of water for 50–60 minutes. Peel the bulbs, cut into small pieces, and purée with some vegetable stock. Peel the horseradish and grate finely. Heat the sour cream with the red beet puree. Stir in the horseradish and the vegetable stock until the desired consistency is reached. Season to taste with salt, pepper, Worcestershire sauce, and sugar.

Whole roasted small potatoes with caraway go well with this recipe.

Chive Egg Butter with Stuffed Peppers

INGREDIENTS: 2 red peppers • 4½ oz mushrooms • 7 oz diced shallots • 1 diced garlic clove • 2 tablespoons sunflower oil • 1 can pizza tomatoes • 1 small can of corn • 4 tablespoons rolled oats • 1 egg • 1 bunch chopped parsley • some dried thyme • salt • freshly ground pepper • 1 cup vegetable stock • 4 tablespoons grated cheese • 2 egg yolks • 2 oz butter • 1 bunch chives

PREPARATION: Halve the peppers lengthwise, remove the seeds and partitions, and wash. Clean the mushrooms and dice. Cook the mushrooms with the shallots and the garlic in hot cooking oil for 2 minutes. Stir the drained corn and oats into the mixture and let thicken until creamy. Cool. Add the egg, parsley, thyme, salt and pepper. Preheat the oven to 400°F. Stuff the peppers halves with the filling and arrange next to each other in a baking dish. Fill the baking dish with broth and cover with aluminum foil. Bake the peppers slowly for 20 minutes. Remove the aluminum foil, sprinkle the cheese over the filling and bake for 10 minutes. Pour the cooking juice into a pot, stir in the egg yolks and butter with a mixing tool but do not simmer. Season the sauce with salt, pepper and chives.

Good with rice or salad potatoes.

Hot Pepper Sauce with Grilled Vegetable Skewers

INGREDIENTS: 4 small onions • 2–3 zucchinis • 1 small eggplant • 8 brown champignons • 1 boiled corn cob • 3 red peppers • 1 yellow pepper • 4 tablespoons olive oil • salt • freshly ground pepper • 2 chopped garlic cloves • 1 green, chili pepper, chopped • 2 tablespoons tomato paste • 4 tablespoons tomato ketchup • 1 teaspoon black bean sauce • 4 tablespoons chopped cilantro

PREPARATION: Peel the onions and halve. Clean the zucchini, eggplant, and champignons, wash, and rub dry. Divide the eggplant and corn on the cob into 8 same-sized large pieces. Dice the rest of the zucchini and eggplant finely. Clean 1 red and 1 yellow pepper, wash and divide into four pieces. Put the vegetables onto 4 long skewers. Mix some oil with the pepper. Spread the mix onto the vegetables and grill until they are soft. Quarter the remaining peppers, clean, and peel. Cut the peppers into narrow strips. For the sauce, stew the diced vegetables, the paprika strips, garlic, and chili in the remaining cooking oil for 2 minutes. Stir in tomato paste and ketchup and thicken lightly until creamy. Puree the sauce coarsely and season to taste with salt, pepper, bean sauce, and cilantro. Serve warm or cold with the vegetable skewers.

TIP

Soak wooden skewers in water before use. Boiled corn on the cob can be bought year round in cans. Black bean sauce is available in Asian specialty food stores.

Anchovy Sauce with Vegetable Sticks

INGREDIENTS: 6 celery stalks • 3 carrots • 1 each red and yellow pepper • 1 fennel bulb • 2 zucchinis • 12 anchovies • 4 peeled garlic cloves • 4 tablespoons capers • 10 tablespoons olive oil • 4 tablespoons butter • 2 tablespoons chopped parsley • pepper

PREPARATION: Wash the celery, peel the carrots, halve the peppers, and core. Halve the fennel also and remove the stalk. Cut the celery, carrots, paprika, fennel, and zucchini in approximately 10 centimeter long pieces. Wrap the vegetables in a damp towel and put in a cool place. Finely chop the anchovies, garlic, and capers separately. Heat 4 tablespoons olive oil and stew the garlic in it until it is transparent. Add the anchovies and let simmer for an additional 2 minutes while constantly stirring. Shortly before serving, stir in the remaining olive oil, capers, and butter and bring to a boil for a short time. Garnish the white, creamy anchovy sauce with chopped parsley, pepper, and some salt. Serve with the vegetables.

Fresh white bread baguettes go well with this recipe.

Garlic Herb Oil with Mediterranean Vegetables

INGREDIENTS: 1 eggplant • 2 zucchinis • 1 red and 1 yellow pepper • 8 oz brown mushrooms • 1 halved garlic bulb • 2 stalks rosemary • 4 stalks thyme • ½ bunch basil • 2 peeled garlic cloves • olive oil • salt • sugar • freshly ground pepper

PREPARATION: Cut the eggplant and zucchini into ⅓ inch thick slices and salt lightly. Preheat the oven to 375°F. Halve the peppers and put the skin side facing up in a frying pan. Add 1 rosemary and 2 thyme leaves, and the garlic halves to the pan and drizzle with 4 tablespoons olive oil. Cook for approximately 30 minutes. Dab the eggplant and zucchini slices with paper towels. Clean the mushrooms. Fry the mushrooms with the eggplant and zucchini in hot cooking oil on both sides until golden brown. Take them out and drain fat onto paper towels. Take the peppers out of the frying pan, skin, and cut into approximately 1 in wide strips. Remove the remaining rosemary and thyme from the stalks and place along with the basil leaves and the peeled garlic cloves in a blender. Add ½ cup olive oil and puree. Season it with salt, sugar and pepper. Brush the eggplant, zucchini, mushrooms and paprika on both sides with the spicy oil and marinate covered for 2 hours. Serve this recipe with fresh white bread.

Béarnaise Sauce with Julienned Vegetables

INGREDIENTS: 1 lb carrots • 2 large potatoes • 1 lb zucchini • 1 tablespoon olive oil • salt • freshly ground pepper • freshly ground nutmeg • 1 packet Béarnaise Sauce • ½ cup butter • 1 teaspoon of chopped tarragon leaves

TIP
You can find various tools in well-stocked household articles stores with which to make vegetable noodles.

PREPARATION: Peel the carrots and the potatoes. Clean the zucchini and wash. Julienne the vegetables and potatoes. Cook in a little water until soft, strain and catch the cooking water. Let the vegetables drain well. Mix the vegetables with oil and season with salt, pepper, and nutmeg. Warm ½ cup vegetable cooking water, stir in the sauce powder with a whisk and simmer for 1 minute. Cut the butter into pieces and stir in gradually. Finally, add the tarragon to the sauce and pour the sauce over the vegetable noodles.

Freshly grated Parmesan goes well with this recipe.

Tomato Onion Sauce with Leeks

INGREDIENTS: 6 medium-sized leeks • salt • 2 table-spoons melted butter • freshly ground pepper • freshly ground nutmeg • ¾ lb peeled onions • 2 chopped garlic cloves • 1 teaspoon crushed corian-der seeds • 2 bay leaves • 2 tablespoons olive oil • 2 cans pizza tomatoes • honey • soy sauce • 2 table-spoons chopped parsley • 1 piece of parmesan

PREPARATION: Clean the leeks and cut away the dark green parts. Wash well and cook slowly in a little salt water for 8–10 minutes. Put the stalks into a bak-ing dish and spread with butter. Sprinkle with salt, pepper, and nutmeg. Keep the vegetables warm. Cut the onions into narrow strips. Put the onions, garlic, corian-der seeds and bay leaves into hot cooking oil until brown. Add tomatoes and thicken the mix uncovered until creamy. Season the sauce to taste with salt, pepper, honey, soy sauce and chopped parsley. Remove the solid spices. Pour the sauce over the leek and heat for a short time in the oven. Grate some Parmesan over it.

Rice with raisins and roasted almond slices goes well with this recipe.

Coconut Curry Sauce with Fennel

INGREDIENTS: 1 lb fennel bulbs • 2 teaspoons butter • ½ teaspoon vegetable stock • ½ lb beef tomatoes • salt • freshly ground pepper • 8 oz Crème Fraiche • 4 oz cream • 1 teaspoon flour • 1 egg yolk • curry • 2 tablespoons highly-concentrated vinegar • sugar • 2 tablespoons chopped chives

PREPARATION: Wash the fennel bulbs, remove greens and cut into 4–5 slices each. Cook slowly in a little salt water with some butter and broth granules for 8 minutes. Drain and reserve broth. Butter a baking dish. Place the fennel in the dish. Wash the tomatoes and cut away the stems. Slice the tomatoes and put them onto the fennel like roofing tiles. Sprinkle with salt and pepper. Preheat the oven to 400°F. Stir in approximately ½ cup fennel broth with Crème Fraiche, cream and flour. Bring to a boil. Stir in the egg yolk and season the sauce to taste with salt, pepper, curry, vinegar and sugar. Pour the sauce over the vegetables and cook slowly in a preheated oven for approximately 15 minutes. Sprinkle with chives before serving. Good with mashed potatoes or rice.

Sour Cream Sauce with Grilled Peppers

INGREDIENTS: 4 red peppers • ¾ cup heavy cream or Crème Fraiche • cayenne pepper • salt • sugar

PREPARATION: Wash the peppers and wipe dry. Roast the peppers in the oven at 500°F for 15–20 minutes turning constantly, so that the skin bursts on all sides. Put the peppers in a porcelain bowl and cover with a plate or lid until they are some-what cooled. Skin the peppers over the bowl so that all the juice is caught. Also remove the top and the seeds. Cut peppers into 5–6 wide strips lengthwise and keep warm in the oven. Mash the skinned pods and tips with a purée tool or strain through a fine strainer. Heat the cream, but do not let it simmer. Season with cayenne pepper, salt, and some sugar before folding in the pepper puree. Pour the sauce out onto a preheated dish. Arrange the warm pepper strips on it.

Warm flat bread and spicy tomato butter goes well with this recipe.

Coconut Cilantro Sauce with Pumpkin

INGREDIENTS: 4 lbs Hokkaido pumpkin • 3½ oz peeled onions • ¾ lb leeks • 2 small, red chili peppers • 3 tablespoons peanut oil • 1 cup vegetable stock • 3 cups coconut milk • 3 teaspoons highly concentrated vinegar • 1 tablespoon crushed coriander seeds • salt • freshly ground pepper • ½ cup cream • 6 tablespoons chopped cilantro

PREPARATION: Quarter the pumpkin. Remove the seeds and soft parts as well as the peel. Cut the pumpkin into equally large cubes. Cut the onions into small pieces. Cut the leeks into rings and wash carefully. Cut the chili peppers into rings. Fry the onions, leeks and chili in 1 tablespoon oil until brown and place on a plate. Add the remaining oil to the pot and sauté the pumpkin rind. Pour the broth into the mix and simmer for 10 minutes. Add coconut milk, highly concentrated vinegar, crushed coriander seeds and the onion-leek mixture to the pumpkin. Whip the cream and mix it with chopped cilantro and stir both into the vegetabl.

Garden Herb Sauce with Small Tofu Balls

INGREDIENTS: 6 small tomatoes • 1 zucchini • 3 large mushrooms • 1 cup vegetable stock • 5 oz smoked tofu • 1 bunch chopped chives • 1 tablespoon medium hot mustard • 2 tablespoons Crème Fraîche • herb salt • 1 bunch parsley • 1 bunch chervil • 2 oz of watercress • 3 leaves of lovage • 1 chopped garlic clove • soy sauce • 4 tablespoons olive oil

PREPARATION: Skin the tomatoes, cut into quarters and remove the seeds. Wrap the tomato pieces in paper towels to dry. Wash the zucchini and cut into 1 inch thick slices. Cut the slices into thirds to form small triangles. Clean the mushrooms and cube. Steam briefly in 1 tablespoon vegetable stock. Stir the mashed smoked tofu, mushroom, chives, mustard and Crème Fraîche together. Season with herb salt. Let sit covered for 1–2 hours. For the sauce, wash the herbs and pat dry. Pick the leaves off the stems. Mix herbs, garlic, soy sauce, herb salt and vegetable stock in a blender. Gradually pour olive oil onto the mixture. Put the herb sauce onto 4 plates. Put 3 round clumps of tofu on each plate. Arrange the quarter slices of tomatoes around the tofu to look like flowers. Put the zucchini triangles between the tomato quarter slices.

Ginger-Shallot Sauce for Sautéed Plum Tomatoes

INGREDIENTS: 1 diced carrot • 1 diced stick of celery • 2 thick peeled cloves of garlic • 5 tablespoons olive oil • 1 bay leaf • 1 stalk of thyme • 1 stalk of rosemary • 1 tablespoon tomato paste • 2 cups tomato juice • salt • freshly ground pepper • sugar • 1 teaspoon freshly grated ginger • 12 shallots • 12 plum tomatoes • 12 mild green chili husks • 2 tablespoons lime juice

> **TIP**
> Chilis have differing levels of spiciness. The sharpness of the pepper can be reduced by separating the seeds from the husks.

PREPARATION: Brown vegetables with garlic in 1 tablespoon oil. Add the bay leaf, thyme, rosemary, tomato paste and tomato juice. Simmer at low heat for 30 minutes. Pass mixture through a sieve and season to taste with salt, pepper, sugar, and ginger. Remove the skin of the shallots and tomatoes. Cut the shallots into eighths lengthwise and cut the stems from the tomatoes. Wash the chili husks. Heat the remaining cooking oil and simmer the shallots in it for 5 minutes. Add tomatoes and chili peppers and simmer 5 more minutes. Add the tomato juice, heat and season with lime juice. Best well-cooled with crispy pita bread.

Green Béchamel Sauce with Green Tomatoes

TIP
During the winter, green and green-orange Italian tomatoes are offered in the market. Small, round and firm, they have a strong fruit flavor and are best for this dish.

INGREDIENTS: 16 green tomatoes • flour • 2–3 eggs • approximately 2 cups breadcrumbs • 4 tablespoons grated parmesan • salt • freshly ground pepper • olive oil • 1 stalk rosemary • 2 peeled garlic cloves • 4 tablespoons butter • 2 tablespoons flour • 1 cup vegetable stock • 1 cup milk • 3 ½ oz young Gouda • freshly grated nutmeg • 3 tablespoons fresh basil leaves • lemon juice • 4 tablespoons chopped pistachios.

PREPARATION: Wash, halve and stem the tomatoes. Slice and let them dry on kitchen paper. Put flour, eggs and breadcrumbs, mixed with parmesan, onto plates. Season the eggs with salt and pepper and a few drops of water. Heat up a lot of cooking oil in a frying pan and flavor with rosemary and garlic. Dust the tomatoes with flour and dip into the eggs and press into the breadcrumbs. Fry until golden-yellow on each side. Heat the butter for the sauce. Cook the flour in it briefly. Pour in the broth with milk and stir until smooth. Let simmer for 10 minutes. Melt the cheese in the sauce. Season with salt, pepper and nutmeg. Crush the basil leaves with some lemon juice. Stir with the pistachios into the sauce and serve with golden-yellow saffron rice.

Peppermint Tomato Sauce with Zucchini Rolls

INGREDIENTS: 2 yellow zucchinis, each 9 oz • 2 green zucchinis each 9 oz • olive oil • salt • freshly ground pepper • 4 tablespoons pine nuts • 6 tablespoons chopped basil • 6 tablespoons chopped parsley • 1 diced shallot • 2 chopped cloves of garlic • 5 oz feta chees • 3½ tablespoons grated Pecorino • 1 cup full fat fresh cheese • 1 tablespoon bread crumbs • 16 oz tomatoes • 1 diced onion • 4 tablespoons chopped peppermint leaves • ½ cup vegetable stock • sugar • 2–3 teaspoons highly concentrated vinegar • 6 sage leaves

PREPARATION: Wash zucchini, and cut each lengthwise into eight slices. Chop ends finely. Fry zucchini slices briefly in oil on both sides. Season with salt and pepper. Dry roast pine nuts in a pan. Chop ¾ of the nuts and mix with herbs, shallots, garlic, cheeses and breadcrumbs to a spreadable consistency. Season. Stack one green and one yellow zucchinni slice, spread with filling, roll up and secure with kitchen string. Peel, core and cube tomatoes. Sautee onion in 3 tablespoons oil, add mint and broth and simmer 10 minutes. Pass through a sieve. Stir in diced zucchini, tomatoes and the remaining pine nuts, bring to a boil and flavor with salt, pepper, sugar and vinegar. Heat zucchini rolls in the sauce for 5 minutes and garnish with sage leaves.

Green Pepper Sauce with Grilled Corn

> **TIP**
> Canned corn cobs are already cooked and can be grilled immediately.

INGREDIENTS: 4 fresh corn cobs • 2 tablespoons melted butter • 1 tablespoon olive oil • 1 chopped shallot • 1 chopped clove of garlic • 7 tablespoons dried vermouth • 3 tablespoons fresh green peppercorn or pickled peppercorn • ½ cups Crème Fraiche • salt • sugar.

PREPARATION: Cook corn cobs slowly for 30 minutes. Drain well. Mix butter and cooking oil and pour the mixture over the corn and grill. For the sauce, cook the shallot, the garlic clove with vermouth and the crushed peppercorns until the mixture becomes thick. Stir in the Crème Fraiche and season to taste with salt and sugar.

Gorgonzola Sauce with Zucchini Flan

INGREDIENTS: 1 green ½ lb zucchini • 1 yellow ½ lb zucchini • butter for form • 1 diced shallot • 1 chopped clove of garlic • 1 tablespoon butter • ½ cup vegetable stock • 1 piece of lemon peel • 2 eggs • 2 egg yolks • 3 tablespoons Crème Fraiche • salt • freshly ground pepper • freshly grated nutmeg • 1 cup cream • 3 ½ oz Gorgonzola.

PREPARATION: Wash the zucchini and wipe dry. Peel 4 large strips of peel from each fruit. Grease 4 small forms and put one green and one yellow strip in a cross-shaped, overlapping manner in the small forms. Cut the vegetables into small pieces. Sauté the shallots and garlic cubes in hot butter. Add zucchini, broth and the lemon peel. Cook until soft, strain and drain well. Remove the lemon peel. Cook the broth until it becomes very thick. Stir in eggs, egg yolk and Crème Fraiche. Mash the zucchini and add to the broth. Season with salt, pepper and nutmeg. Preheat the oven to 400°F. Pour the zucchini mixture into the small forms. Put the peeled strips over them and cover with tin foil. Let the small forms cook slowly in bain-marie in an oven for 25–30 minutes. Heat up the cream and melt Gorgonzola slowly into it. Season. Loosen each flan around the edge with a knife, turn upside down onto a plate and decorate with the Gorgonzola sauce.

Brandy Olive Sauce with Eggs

INGREDIENTS: 8 eggs • 1lb tomatoes • 2 chopped onions • 3 tablespoons tomato paste • 2 tablespoons paprika paste • 1 tablespoons mild mustard • 1–2 teaspoons highly concentrated vinegar • 8 black olives without pits • 8 stuffed green olives • 3 tablespoons brandy • 3 tablespoons white wine • salt • freshly ground pepper • 1 teaspoon sugar • cayenne pepper.

PREPARATION: Cook the eggs until they are as soft as wax, rinse under cold water and peel. Put the tomatoes into boiling water for a short time, peel and take out the seeds. Mash the tomato pulp and mix the onions, tomato paste, paprika puree, mustard and concentrated vinegar well. Chop the olives coarsely. Put brandy and white wine into the tomato mixture, stir well and season until spicy with salt, pepper, sugar and cayenne pepper. Put the eggs in the sauce and let them sit for at least 3 hours in the refrigerator. Fresh white bread and a bowl of salad go well with this meal.

Herb Bacon Sauce with Eggs

INGREDIENTS: 4 oz bacon • 4 diced shallots • 1 peeled garlic clove • 5 tablespoons butter • 3 tablespoons flour • 1 cup vegetable stock • 1 cup cream • 2 tablespoons highly concentrated vinegar • 1 bunch each: chives, parsley and dill • salt • freshly ground pepper • freshly grated nutmeg • 1 tablespoon sugar • 8 eggs.

PREPARATION: Cut the bacon into very fine cubes and heat it moderately. Stir in the shallots, the press garlic and melt the butter into it. Let everything cook for a short time until brown. Stir in the flour and add the broth and cream. Stir the sauce until smooth and let simmer for 10 minutes. Put the highly concentrated vinegar into the sauce. Wash the herbs, spin dry and chop finely. Chop the chives. Put the herbs into the sauce. Season to taste with salt, pepper, nutmeg and sugar. Boil the eggs until they are soft as wax, peel and let stand 5 minutes in the sauce. Mashed potatoes go well with this meal.

Sauces for Pasta

What is better than a plate of steaming hot pasta and an aromatic sauce made of sun-ripened tomatoes? And to go with it freshly grated Parmigiano Reggiano and a bottle of old Chianti Classico. The most beloved pasta sauces are tomato sauce and Bolognese Sauce. A perfect example of how exquisite pasta tastes with vegetables is the excellent recipe for Orecchiette with Broccoli and Red Onions. Green Tagliatelle Noodles (ribbon noodles) with Wild Boar Ragout and Porcini Mushrooms are exquisite. Sage and Ham Butter Sauce with Spinach and Goat Cheese Noodels is superb, as is Forest Mushroom Sauce with Grilled Polenta or Eggplant-Mint Sauce with linguini. Gnocchi (thick, round Italian potato noodles) in fruity herb sauce and Cucumber-Shrimp-Sauce with black fettuccini round out this chapter.

Pasta Primavera

INGREDIENTS: 1 lb green tagliatella (ribbon noodles) • salt
• 1 bunch spring onions • 2 carrots • 1 lb asparagus heads
• 3½ oz frozen peas • sugar • freshly ground pepper
• 3½ oz butter • 4 tablespoons chopped chervil • 3½ tablespoons grated parmesan

PREPARATION: Bring a lot of water to a boil, salt generously and let the noodles cook slowly until they are soft. Wash
the spring onions and chop the lighter parts finely. Cut the
dark parts into small rolls and put to the side. Peel the carrots and asparagus and cut into slices or small pieces. Let

the peas thaw. Cook the vegetables slowly
in a little bit of salt water until soft. Cook the
butter until it is lightly brown and season
with salt and pepper. Stir in the vegetables.
Strain the noodles and put into a warm
bowl. Fold in the buttered vegetables with
the chervil. Sprinkle the cheese over it.

Radicchio Mushroom Sauce with Tagliatelle

INGREDIENTS: 1 lb Tagliatelle (ribbon noodles) • salt • 1 radicchio • 10 ½ oz brown mushrooms • 2 tablespoons olive oil • 1 cup milk • 2 small packages lightly-colored sauce • 3 ½ oz grated gouda • freshly grated nutmeg • freshly ground pepper • 2 tablespoons chopped basil

PREPARATION: Bring plenty of water to a boil, salt generously and cook the tagliatelle until soft. Clean the radicchio, halve, cut into thin strips and put a few strips to the side. Clean the mushrooms and slice. Cook the mushrooms in oil for 1 minute. Add the radicchio, milk and one cup of water. Stir in the sauce powder and bring to a boil. Grate the cheese finely and melt in the hot, not boiling sauce. Season with salt, pepper and nutmeg. Stir in the basil. Strain the tagliatelle, mix with the sauce and spread fresh radicchio strips over it

Tomato Sauce with Spaghetti

INGREDIENTS: 1 lb spaghetti • salt • 1 chopped onion • 2 chopped garlic cloves • 2 lbs tomatoes • 2 tablespoons olive oil • 2 tablespoons tomato paste • 1 bay leaf • freshly ground pepper • 1 teaspoon honey • 1 tablespoons balsamic vinegar • 2 tablespoons chopped herbs (parsley, basil, oregano, thyme) • 2 tablespoons butter • ½ cup grated parmesan

PREPARATION: Bring plenty of water to a boil, salt generously and cook the spaghetti slowly until it is soft. Sauté the onion and garlic in hot oil until brown. Wash the tomatoes, cut off the stems, cut into quarters and add along with the tomato paste and bay leaf to the onions. Let the tomatoes simmer in a closed pot for 5 minutes. Stir often. Fish out the tomato skins with

a fork. Let the sauce cook until it has a consistency of light cream. Season to taste with salt, pepper, honey, balsamic vinegar and chopped herbs. Drain the spaghetti, mix with butter and serve with the sauce. Serve with ample amounts of freshly grated parmesan.

Aurora Spaghetti Sauce

INGREDIENTS: 1 lb spaghetti • salt • 7 oz chopped shallots • 2 chopped garlic cloves • 3 tablespoons olive oil• ½ cup dry vermouth • ½ cup dry white wine • 2 bay leaves • 1 piece of lemon peel • 4 stalks of thyme • 2 stalks rosemary • 6 tomatoes • 1 cup cream • salt • freshly ground pepper • 1 bunch basil • 5 tablespoons grated Pecorino cheese.

PREPARATION: Bring an ample amount of water to a boil, salt generously and cook the spaghetti until soft. Cook the shallots and garlic until brown in 2 tablespoons cooking oil. Add the vermouth, wine, bay leaves, lemon peel, thyme, and rosemary. Boil uncovered until reduced to ½ cup. Rub sauce through sieve. Cut the stems off the tomatoes, place for a short time in boiling water, skin, take out the seeds and cut into cubes. Pour the cream into the vegetable juice and cook until thick. Stir in the tomatoes and season with salt and pepper. Pluck the basil from the stem and mix into the sauce. Strain the spaghetti, mix with the remaining cooking oil, add the sauce and serve with grated Pecorino.

Eggplant Mint Sauce with Linguine

TIP
Cooking pasta isn't difficult at all. Each ½ cup can be brought to a boil with 1 quart water. Salt generously and shake the noodles in carbonated water. When cooking slowly, the water should bubble more. Even if the cooking time is given on the package, you should check the noodles yourself to make sure they have reached the desired softness.

INGREDIENTS: 1 lb linguine • salt • 1 lb eggplant • 6 tablespoons olive oil • 4 spring onions • 4 garlic cloves • 1 red chili pepper • ½ yellow bell pepper • 1 tablespoon tomato paste • 1¼ cups tomato sauce • 1 can pizza tomatoes • 3 bay leaves • 10 peppermint leaves • freshly ground pepper • 2 tablespoons butter • ½ cup grated parmesan.

PREPARATION: Bring an ample amount of water to a boil, salt generously and cook the linguine in it until it is solf. Clean the eggplant, wash, rub dry and cut into very small cubes. Sprinkle with salt and drip 2 tablespoons cooking oil over it. Clean the spring onions, garlic, chili pepper and bell pepper. Peel if necessary, remove the seeds and cut into fine cubes. Heat the remaining cooking oil and cook the onions, garlic, chili, and bell pepper for a short time until brown. Add the eggplant cubes, tomato juice, pizza tomatoes and bay leaves and allow mixture to thicken until creamy. Cut the peppermint leaves into strips. Drain the linguine and mix with butter. Season the sauce to taste with salt, pepper and mint. Mix with the linguine.

Paprika Zucchini Sauce with Pappardelle

INGREDIENTS: 1 lb of Pappardelle • salt • 2 small zucchinis • 3 paprika husks (red, yellow and green) • 2 peeled garlic cloves • 4 tablespoons of olive oil • 1 chopped chili husk • some grated lemon peel • 4 tablespoons of tomato ketchup • 1 teaspoon of fresh thyme leaves • 1 teaspoon of chopped rosemary • ½ cup of red wine • freshly ground pepper • 2 tablespoons of butter • ½ cup of grated Fontina cheese

TIP
Paprika husks can be easily peeled with a sharp paning tool. Grill halved husks for 30 minutes or until the skin is black. Put a moist towel over them and the skin will easily shed itself.

PREPARATION: Boil ample amount of salted water and cook the Pappardelle in it until soft. Dice washed zucchini. Halve bell peppers, remove seeds, peel and cut into small cubes. Add pressed garlic to hot cooking oil. Stir in chili, diced vegetables, lemon peel, ketchup, thyme, rosemary and red wine. Simmer vegetable sauce in covered pot on medium heat for 20 minutes. Season with salt and pepper. Strain Pappardelle and mix with butter. Put the sauce on the Pappardelle and serve with freshly grated cheese.

Garlic Olive Oil Sauce with Capellini

INGREDIENTS: 4 peeled garlic cloves • 4 dried chili peppers • 1 lb Capellini • salt • 6 tablespoons (olive oil • freshly ground pepper • 6 tablespoons butter • 6 tablespoons chopped basil

PREPARATION: Cut the garlic into thin slices. Chop the chili peppers in a mortar or with a knife. The seeds of the small husks are very hot. For those who do not like spicy foods: cut the husks into halves and remove the seeds from the mashed husks. Bring an ample amount of water to a boil and salt generously. Cook the capellini slowly until soft. At the same time, heat the olive oil and cook the garlic until brown. Add chili. Strain the Capellini and add olive oil. Season with salt and pepper and enhance the flavor with butter and basil.

Creamy Peach and Cheese Sauce with Farfalle

INGREDIENTS: 2 large, ripe peaches • 1 peeled shallot • 1 peeled garlic clove • 4 tablespoons butter • 1 lb cream • 1 lb grated gouda • some white wine • 1 lb Farfalle • salt • freshly ground pepper • ½ bunch basil

TIP
Use 7 oz fresh or boiled shrimp or the same amount of cooked diced ham instead of peaches.

PREPARATION: Halve and pit the peaches. Then cut into small cubes. Place peach cubes into boiling water for a short time and the skin will peel off easily. Cut the shallots and garlic into small pieces and sauté in 2 tablespoons butter. Pour in cream and bring almost to a boil. Stir the cheese into the hot, but not boiling, cream. Season to taste with white wine. Bring an ample amount of water to a boil, salt generously and let the Farfalle cook slowly until soft. Strain the noodles and mix with the leftover butter. Heat the peach cubes in the sauce and season to taste with salt and pepper. Remove the stems from the basil leaves and cut into strips. Mix the Farfalle with the sauce and basil.

Broccoli Onion Sauce with Orecchiette

INGREDIENTS: 1 lb broccoli • salt • 4 red onions • 1 bunch Italian dandelion leaves • 1 lb of Orecchiette • 4 tablespoons olive oil • 2 peeled garlic cloves • 2 tablespoons butter • ½ cup cream • 1 dried chili pepper • freshly ground pepper • 3 ½ tablespoons grated parmesan

PREPARATION: Take the leaves and thick stem from the broccoli. Peel the stem and cut into small pieces. Halve the small flowerets or cut into quarters according to size. Cook them in boiling water until soft and pour into a strainer. Rinse in ice-cold water. Halve the red onions and cut into strips. Remove the dandelion leaves from stem and cut into bite-sized pieces. Wash thoroughly and spin-dry. Bring an ample amount of water to a boil, salt generously and cook the Orecchiette slowly until soft. Strain the Orecchiette, but save the noodle water. Sauté the onions in 2 tablespoons olive oil until transparent. Add broccoli and garlic and let fry slowly for an additional 5 minutes. Add the dandelion and Orecchiette and pour in a few spoonfuls of noodle water. Add the remaining olive oil, butter, and cream and shake to coat. Season with salt, chili and pepper. Serve freshly grated parmesan separately.

Feta Parsley Sauce with Penne

INGREDIENTS: 1 lb penne • salt • 3 ½ tablespoons pine nuts • ½ cup feta • ½ cup Crème Fraîche • 4 peeled garlic cloves • 1 bunch chopped parsley • some grated lemon peel • 2 chopped chili peppers (green and red) • ½ lb plum tomatoes • 2 grilling sausages • 3 ½ oz peeled shallots • 2 tablespoons olive oil • 2 tablespoons fresh thyme leaf • 2 tablespoons butter

PREPARATION: Bring an ample amount of water to a boil and salt generously. Cook penne in it slowly until soft. Roast pine nuts in pan without cooking oil until lightly brown. Crush feta cheese and stir until smooth with the Crème Fraîche. Press garlic into it and add chopped parsley, lemon peel and chili husks. Strain penne and save water. Stir feta cream with noodle cooking water until creamy. Wash tomatoes, off stems and halve. Make little balls out of grilled sausages. Cut onions into narrow strips. Fry small balls in hot cooking oil for 3 minutes. Add onions and tomatoes and let simmer an additional 5 minutes. Season with salt and pepper. Mix hot penne with butter and sausage-onion-tomato mixture. Pour hot feta-parsley-sauce over it and sprinkle it with pine nuts and thyme leaves.

TIP

Instead of feta, the sauce can also be prepared with the same amount of Gorgonzola or Roquefort. If you buy lamb sausage instead of the pork, cut it into slices and fry it until crispy in olive oil.

Chanterelle Sauce with Tagliatelle

INGREDIENTS: 1 lb green asparagus • salt • 4 tablespoons butter • ½ lb of tagliatelle (ribbon noodles) • 8 slices of smoked ham • 1 lb chanterelle moshrooms • 1 peeled shallot • 1 stalk of thyme • 4 tablespoons olive oil • 1 cup cream • freshly ground pepper • ½ cup parmesan

PREPARATION: Peel the asparagus, remove the woody ends, halve the stems lengthwise, and cook slowly for 10 minutes in lightly boiling salt water. Take them out, strain, and keep warm on the stove top in a casserole with 1 tablespoon butter. Bring an ample amount of water to a boil, salt generously and cook the tagliatelle in it until soft. Cut the ham into strips. Clean the chanterelles, cut the shallots into small pieces, pick off the thyme and cook everything together for 5–8 minutes in the remaining butter. Pour cream into it. Strain the tagliatelle, let drain and serve together with the asparagus and the chanterelles. Place the strips of ham over the pasta. Drizzle with olive oil, add salt and pepper and strew with freshly grated parmesan.

Spaghetti Bolognese

INGREDIENTS: 2 stalks celery • 1 carrot • 2 onions • 3 garlic cloves • 2 ½ cups mixed ground meat • salt • freshly ground pepper • 4 tablespoons olive oil • 2 tablespoons tomato paste • 1 can tomatoes (3½ cups) • 1 stalk rosemary • 1 stalk thyme • 1 lb spaghetti • 2 tablespoons butter • ½ teaspoon oregano • cayenne pepper • ½ cup grated parmesan

PREPARATION: Clean and peel the celery and the carrot. Peel the onions and garlic and cut everything into small cubes. Season the ground meat with salt and pepper and fry until crumbly in hot olive oil. Add chopped vegetables, onions, garlic and tomato paste and let simmer 5 minutes. Stir constantly. Drain the tomatoes in a strainer and save the juice. Chop the tomatoes coarsely and add them, along with the juice and fresh herbs, to the ground meat. Let simmer for approximately one hour in a covered pot at low heat. Stir continually. Bring an ample amount of water to a boil, salt generously and cook the spaghetti in it. Pour into a strainer, let drain and mix with butter. Season the sauce with oregano, salt, pepper, and cayenne pepper and pour onto the spaghetti. Serve with freshly grated parmesan.

Amatriciana Sauce with Bevette

INGREDIENTS: 3 peeled onions • 2 peeled garlic cloves
• 7 oz bacon • 6 tomatoes • 2 tablespoons olive oil
• 1 can pizza tomatoes • salt • freshly ground pepper
• 1 lb Bevette • 4 tablespoons chopped smooth parsley
• 2 hard-boiled eggs • ½ cup grated parmesan

PREPARATION: Halve the onions and cut into strips. Chop the garlic finely. Cut the bacon into thin strips. Remove the stems from the tomatoes and put into boiling water. Use a skimmer to remove the tomatoes and rinse in ice-cold water. Then remove the skins. Cut the tomatoes into quarters, remove the seeds and cut them into strips. Let the onions and bacon fry in olive oil until brown and pour the pizza tomatoes over all. Simmer slowly for 15 minutes, then add the tomato strips and flavor with salt. Bring an ample amount of water to boil, salt generously and cook bevette until soft. Strain the noodles and save some of the noodle water. Mix the bevette with onion sauce, add a few spoonfuls of noodle water and round out with some chopped parsley. Serve on a plate and sprinkle with chopped egg and parmesan.

Wild Boar Ragout with Tagliatelle

INGREDIENTS: 1 lb wild boar shoulder • salt • freshly ground pepper • 2 tablespoons cooking oil • 1 peeled carrot • ¼ peeled celery root • 4 peeled onions • 2 tablespoons tomato paste • 5 peppercorns • 2 allspice berriens • 5 juniper berries • 2 cloves • 1 bay leaf • 1 cup red wine • 3 cups beef stock • 1 ½ cups wide green tagliatelle (ribbon noodles) • 1 cup porcini • 2 tablespoons butter • 1 diced shallot • 4 tablespoons parsley

PREPARATION: Cut the meat into fine cubes. Salt and pepper and fry in oil. Cut the carrot, celery, and onions into fine cubes and cook in tomato paste for 5 minutes. Preheat the oven to 350°F. Grind the seasoning coarsely and season the meat. Pour in some red wine and reduce the liquid. Repeat. Pour in 2 cups broth and simmer covered for 2 ½ hours in the oven. After approximately 1 hour, pour the remaining broth into the mix. Take out the pieces of meat, strain the sauce through a fine strainer and season with salt and pepper. Chop the pieces of meat into smaller pieces and put them into the sauce. Bring the remaining water to a boil, salt generously and cook the noodles in it slowly until they are soft, then strain. Clean the porcini and cut into strips. Fry in hot butter until brown on both sides. Add one shallot and shake briefly to coat. Mix the tagliatelle noodles with the ragout and porcini.

Bucatini alla Carbonara

INGREDIENTS: 7 oz bacon • 1 onion • 1 lb bucatini • salt • 2 tablespoons of olive oil • 1 cup cream • 6 egg yolks • 7 tablespoons parmesan • freshly ground pepper.

PREPARATION: Chop the bacon into cubes. Peel the onions and cut into small cubes. Bring an ample amount of water to a boil, salt generously and let the bucatini cook slowly until soft. Pour it into a strainer and let drain. Meanwhile, fry the bacon and onion cubes in a large, heated frying pan with olive oil at low heat until transparent. Mix the cream with egg yolks and 2 tablespoons parmesan and season with salt and pepper.

Mix the hot pasta with bacon and onions and pour the cream sauce over it. Heat up for a short time and stir constantly. Make sure the sauce does not cook otherwise the egg yolks will curdle. Season the pasta with black pepper to taste. Serve the remaining parmesan separately.

Cucumber Shrimp Sauce with Black Fettuccini

INGREDIENTS: 1 lb black fettuccini • salt • 1 cucumber
• 2 peeled garlic cloves • 2 peeled shallots • 4 tablespoons
butter • 1 chopped red chili pepper • 9 oz mascarpone
• 4 tablespoons lemon juice • cayenne pepper • 4 tablespoons chopped dill • sugar • 9 oz boiled, peeled shrimp
• 10 black olives without pits • 7 tablespoons shredded
Greyère

PREPARATION: Bring an ample amount of water to a boil,
salt generously and cook the fettuccini in it slowly until
soft. Peel the cucumber, cut into fourths lengthwise and
remove the seeds. Cut into ⅓ in cubes. Dice the garlic and
shallots finely and fry until brown in 2 tablespoons hot butter. Add the diced cucumbers
and simmer 5 minutes. Stir in the chili and
mascarpone and cook slowly for an additional 5 minutes. Season to taste with salt,
lemon juice, cayenne pepper, dill and sugar.
Strain the fettuccine and season with butter.
Add the shrimp to the sauce and heat again.
Cut the olives into narrow strips and mix with
the sauce. Mix the sauce with the fettuccine
and serve freshly grated cheese separately.

TIP
If you don't like shrimp, use the
same amount of chanterelles instead.
Cook for a short time in butter and
then mix with the finished mascarpone sauce.

Crayfish Sauce with Pasta

TIP
Shrimp can be heated in this strong crayfish sauce and added to any pasta you like.

INGREDIENTS: 1 lb freshwater crayfish shrimp and king shrimp shells • 3½ tablespoons butter • 1 bunch soup greens • 2 peeled onions • 2 peeled cloves of garlic • 1 tablespoon tomato paste • 1 can pizza tomatoes • 2 bay leaves • 2 stalks thyme • 2 stalks rosemary • 1 piece lemon peel • ½ teaspoon fennel seed • 1 teaspoon peppercorns • 1 teaspoon pimiento seeds • 1 teaspoon coriander • ½ cup white wine • ½ cup white port wine • salt • freshly ground pepper

INGREDIENTS: Spread the crayfish shells on a baking sheet and dry out in the oven for 2 hours at 250ºF heat. Melt the

butter and fry the crayfish shells for 3 minutes. Clean the soup greens, peel if necessary and dice finely. Cut the onions and the garlic into small pieces. Add to the crayfish shells and fry well. Add tomato paste, pizza tomatoes, all the spices and herbs, white wine, port wine and 4 cups water and simmer for one hour without a cover. Strain and boil down to the desired consistency. Season with salt and pepper.

Sage and Ham Butter Sauce with Spinach and Goat Cheese Gnocchi

INGREDIENTS: 1 lb fresh spinach • salt • 3½ oz fresh goat cheese • 2 eggs • freshly grated nutmeg • freshly ground pepper • 6 tablespoons crumbled white bread • 6 tablespoons grated parmesan • 7 tablespoons flour • 7 tablespoons butter • 8 slices thinly cut Parma ham • 2 stalks sage

PREPARATION: Clean the spinach and blanch in boiling water. Drain and put into ice-cold water. Let drain, press out well and chop finely. Mix the goat cheese with spinach leaves and eggs and season to taste with salt, nutmeg and pepper. Work in the crumbled white bread, parmesan and flour. Stir into a smooth dough. With two spoons scoop out gnocchi and cook in boiling water for approximately 4 minutes. Let the butter become frothy and let the strips of cut Parma ham and the sage leaves cook until brown. Take the gnocchi out of the water with a skimmer, put on a plate and pour the hot butter and ham over it.

TIP
Goat cheese is not for everyone. You can also use full-fat cheese with or without herbs.

Tomato Red Wine Sauce with Tortelloni and Salami

INGREDIENTS: 1½ lbs fresh Tortelloni with cheese filling • salt • 2 bell peppers (red and green) • ½ lb red onions • 2 peeled garlic cloves • 2 tablespoons olive oil • 1 cup red wine • ½ cup Port wine • 2 bay leaves • 1 can pizza tomatoes • 1 teaspoon paprika • ½ cup of cream • freshly ground pepper • 3½ oz of fennel salami in thin slices • ½ lb buffalo mozzarella • ½ bunch oregano

PREPARATION: Bring an ample amount of water to a boil, salt generously and cook the tortelloni until soft. Peel the bell peppers and cut into very fine strips. Also cut the onions in thin strips and crush the garlic in a presser. Heat the olive oil and cook the paprika, onions and garlic in it until brown. Add red wine, port wine and bay leaves and boil down two thirds. Add tomatoes, paprika powder and cream and bring to a boil. Preheat the oven to 400°F. Grease baking dish. Drain the tortelloni and put into the baking dish. Pour the tomato mixture into it. Lay the slices of salami around the noodles. Slice mozarella and arrange over tortelloni. Sprinkle with salt, pepper, and a few oregano leaves. Brown for 25–30 minutes in a preheated oven. Finally, sprinkle with the remaining fresh oregano leaves.

Tamarillo Tomato Sauce for Ravioli

INGREDIENTS: 1½ lb fresh ravioli with spinach • salt
• 5 tamarillos • ¾ lb tomatoes • 2 diced shallots
• 4 tablespoons butter • 1½ cup red wine • 1 tablespoon
pickled green peppercorns • freshly ground pepper
• 3 tablespoons pine nuts • 1 stalk rosemary • ½ cup grated Fontina

PREPARATION: Bring a lot of water to a boil and salt generously. Cook the ravioli (following the cooking directions)
until soft. Peel the tamarillos and dice finely. Put the tomatoes into the boiling water for a short time, skin, remove the
seeds and cut into small pieces. Cook the shallots in
2 tablespoons butter until brown. Combine the tomatoes,
tamarillo, wine and the shallots and boil rapidly 10 minutes.
Strain the sauce. Stir the remaining butter and peppercorns
into the sauce and season to taste with salt and pepper. Drain
the ravioli and mix with the sauce. Let the pine nuts roast
lightly. Sprinkle the pine nuts and bits of rosemary over the
ravioli.

Serve with freshly grated Fontina cheese.

Asparagus Tarragon Sauce with Ravioli

INGREDIENTS: 1½ lbs asparagus • salt • sugar • 4 tablespoons butter • 2 chopped shallots • 5 tablespoons diced bacon • 6 tablespoons white wine vinegar • 4 tablespoons asparagus stock • 2 egg yolks • 2 tbsp olive oil• 4 tablespoons chopped tarragon • cayenne pepper• 8 cherry tomatoes • 1½ lbs fresh ravioli with meat filling • grated parmesan

PREPARATION: Peel asparagus cut away stringy ends. Cut the asparagus stalks into 3 cm pieces. Boil asparagus in 4 cups water with salt, 1 pinch sugar, 1 teaspoon butter for 8 minutes. Sauté shalots and bacon in 2 tablespoons butter. Pour in white wine vinegar and asparagus stock and boil again. Mix egg yolks with 2 tablespoons warm water until creamy. Strain sauce into egg yolks. Season to taste with remaining butter, olive oil, tarragon, salt and cayenne pepper. Drain asparagus. Cut the stems of plum tomatoes and quarter. Add to sauce with asparagus. Bring water to a boil, salt generously and cook ravioli in it. Drain well. Heat sauce again and mix with ravioli. Serve with freshly grated parmesan.

Sage Walnut Butter with Ravioli

INGREDIENTS: 1½ lbs fresh ravioli with ricotta filling • salt • 1 bunch fresh sage • 8 tablespoons walnut oil • 1 peeled shallot • 1 peeled garlic clove • 15 finely chopped walnuts • 1 untreated lemon • 5 tablespoons butter • 3 ½ oz smoked salmon • 3 ½ tablespoons grated parmesan

PREPARATION: Boil an ample amount of water and season generously. Put half of the sage stalks into the boiling water and cook the ravioli in it slowly until soft. Remove the stems from the remaining sage leaves. Heat half of the walnut oil.

TIP
A variety of freshly prepared ravioli, tortelloni and other pasta specialties are offered in Italian delicatessen shops. Ravioli and tortelloni can also be found in the freezer section of grocery stores.

Dice the shallot and garlic finely and brown in the pan. Add the sage leaves and coarsely chopped walnuts. Wash the lemon in hot water, wipe dry and grate half of the peel into the walnuts. Squeeze the lemon. Mix the juice with the remaining oil and the butter and add them to the sage-nut-butter mixture. Cut the smoked salmon into narrow strips. Drain the ravioli, pour the hot sage-nut-butter mixture over it and mix with the salmon strips. Serve freshly grated parmesan separately.

Wild Mushroom Sauce with Grilled Polenta

INGREDIENTS: 1 cup milk • 1 cup chicken broth • 6 table-spoons garlic butter • salt • freshly grated nutmeg • 10½ tablespoons corn meal • 1 egg • 1 egg yolk • 3½ ozs chopped shallots • 2 chopped garlic cloves • 4 table-spoons butter • 1 cup chanterelle • 1 cup of porcini mushrooms • 1 tablespoon fresh thyme leaf • 4 tablespoons Crème Fraîche

PREPARATION: Heat up the milk with the broth and 2 table-spoons garlic butter. Season to taste generously with salt and nutmeg. Stir in the corn meal. Cook the polenta slowly while continually stirring. Add 1 egg and 1 egg yolk. Grease a baking pan and spread the polenta on it thickly. Cook the shallots and the garlic until brown in half of the butter. Clean the mushrooms and cut into small pieces. Add them to the shallots and cook 3 minutes. Stir in the remaining butter, thyme and Crème Fraiche. Season with salt and pepper. Cut the cooled polenta into rectangles and grill on each side for 3–4 minutes. Cut the remaining garlic butter in slices and divide it among the polenta slices. Serve the mushroom sauce separately.

> **TIP**
> The polenta slices can also be fried in hot olive oil or in rosting fat using a frying pan.

Gorgonzola Pear Sauce with Gnocchi

INGREDIENTS: 1 lb boiling potatoes • 3 ½ tablespoons potato starch • 2 tablespoons soft grain oats • 1 egg yolk • salt • freshly ground pepper • freshly grated nutmeg • flour for kneading • 1 cup cream • ½ cup Gorgonzola cheese • 1 pear • lemon juice • 4 tablespoons fresh marjoram

PREPARATION: Boil the potatoes with their skins until soft, then peel and mash. Mix with the starch, oats and egg yolk. Season with salt, pepper and nutmeg. Roll the potato dough into an approximately 1 inch thick cylinder on a floured working surface and cut into small, thick slices. Press these slices slightly apart from each other with a fork. Bring enough water to a boil, salt generously and cook the gnocchi in it slowly until they start to float on the suface. Heat the cream for the sauce and let the cheese melt in it. Wash the pear, cut into quarters, pit and cut into narrow strips. Add them to the sauce and season to taste with salt, pepper and lemon juice. Drain the gnocchi and pour the sauce on it. Then spread the marjoram over it.

Salad Dressings

The easiest salad dressing consists of a good vinegar, first-rate oil, salt and pepper. The times in which consumers only had red or white wine vinegar and tasteless oil in their kitchen cabinets are long gone. Gourmets today can choose from apple, sherry, raspberry, elderberry cherry and champagne vinegars and many others. Last, but not least, are the beloved spice vinegars from Medina, Acetone Balsamic and balsamic vinegar. Numerous cooking oils spoil us with fine nut flavor and the selection of mild, fruity and spicy olive oils is large. Also try poppy seed oil, linseed oil and sweet almond oil.

Strawberry Almond Dressing with Asparagus Strawberry Salad

TIP
Almond purée and almond oil can be found in health food and whole food shops.

INGREDIENTS: 1½ lbs green asparagus • salt • sugar • 1 teaspoon butter • ⅔ lb strawberries • 5–6 tablespoons strawberry vinegar • 2 tablespoons almond purée • 4 tablespoons almond oil • freshly ground pepper • 1 tablespoon chopped almonds

PREPARATION: Peel only the bottom part of the asparagus and cut away the stringy ends. Boil 1 quart water with salt, 1 pinch sugar and butter. Let asparagus stalks cook for 8 minutes in mixture. Take out asparagus and lay on flat saucer. Save asparagus water. Clean strawberries and drain well. Cut ½ cup strawberries into small pieces and mix with 1 tablespoon sugar. Mash. Cut remaining strawberries into quarters and add them to asparagus. Combine vinegar and almond purée along with

almond oil and some of asparagus cooking water. Stir until creamy. Season to taste with salt and pepper and pour over asparagus and strawberries. Ladle mashed strawberries over all. Finally, sprinkle dish with the chopped almonds.

Raspberry Vinaigrette with Watercress Salad

INGREDIENTS: 1 lb turkey cutlets • salt • freshly ground pepper • 3 tablespoons sunflower oil • lemon and orange peel (1 pinch of each) • 4 oz watercress • 3 tablespoons raspberry vinegar • 2 tablespoons water • 2 tablespoons walnut oil • sugar • 12 raspberries • 1 tablespoon butter

PREPARATION: Cut the meat into narrow strips and season with salt and pepper. Marinate in 1 tablespoon sunflower oil, lemon and orange peel for approximately 15 minutes. Clean the watercress, wash and drain well. Combine the vinegar, water, walnuts and the remaining sunflower oil and season with salt, pepper and one pinch of sugar. Stir the raspberries carefully into the vinaigrette. Heat the butter in a coated frying pan and fry the turkey slowly until golden brown. Serve the watercress with the fried turkey breast strips and pour raspberry vinaigrette over it.

Orange Dressing with Asparagus and Sugar Pea Salad

INGREDIENTS: 1 lb asparagus • 1 cup sugar peas • salt • 1 tablespoon butter • sugar • 4 oz cooked ham • 4 tablespoons pumpkin seed • 2 organic oranges • 4 tablespoons lemon juice • freshly ground pepper • 8 tablespoons olive oil • 1 handful wild garlic or chervil.

PREPARATION: Peel the asparagus carefully and cut into bite-sized pieces. Clean the sugar peas and cut into halves. Place in salt water with butter and a little bit of sugar and cook slowly until soft. Drain and reserve some of the broth. Cut the ham into small strips. Roast the pumpkin seeds in a dry pan. Wash the oranges with hot water, dry and peel fruit. Squeeze out the juice over a bowl. Stir the orange juice, lemon juice, salt, pepper, oil and a little bit of the water used to cook the asparagus until the mixture become creamy. Arrange the asparagus, sugar peas, meat strips, pumpkin seeds and orange slices on a plate. Pour the dressing over the food and sprinkle the strips of orange peel on top. Add a pinch of wild garlic or chervil as well.

TIP

Fresh wild garlic is offered at the weekly market in springtime. Nature lovers can find the aromatic herb in moist soil. But please don't confuse them with lillies of the valley! Wild garlic can be recognized by its garlic smell.

Parmesan Dressing with Potato Asparagus Salad

INGREDIENTS: 2 lbs potatoes • 1 lb green asparagus • salt • ½ beef stock cube • 1 onion • 1 hard boiled egg • 3 tablespoons garlic vinegar • 6 tablespoons olive oil • freshly ground pepper • 4 tablespoons grated parmesan • 1 bunch parsley

PREPARATION: Wash the potatoes and boil, unskinned, for 25 minutes in water. Wash the asparagus, peel the lower parts, and let them cook slowly in 1 cup boiling saltwater for 8 minutes until soft. Take them out of the water and strain them. Bring the asparagus water to a boil again, let the beef stock cube dissolve in it and pour the mixture over the finely chopped onion. Peel and cut the hard-boiled egg into cubes and mix it with the onion in a salad bowl. Mix the vinegar, oil, salt, pepper and parmesan to make a marinade and pour it into the salad bowl. Mix everything thoroughly. Peel and cut the potatoes into thin slices and put them, while still warm, into the marinade. Mix the washed, finely chopped parsley, asparagus, and potatoes together and let sit for 30 minutes.

Honey Dressing with Tomato Arugola Salad

INGREDIENTS: 1 ½ lb cherry tomatoes • 2 tablespoons honey • 6 lemon juice • 2 tablespoons balsamic vinegar • 4 tablespoons almond oil • 4 tablespoons sunflower oil • salt • freshly ground pepper • 2 spring onions • 4 tablespoons sliced almonds • 1 bunch arugola • 4 large peeled garlic cloves • 1 tablespoon butter • 1 teaspoon olive oil

PREPARATION: Stir the honey together with lemon juice, balsamic vinegar, both types of oil, salt and plenty of pepper until creamy. Clean the spring onions and cut into very fine slices. Roast the almond leaves in a frying pan without cooking oil until they become yellow-gold. Wash the tomatoes and arugola. Cut the stems out of the tomatoes and cut the fruit into fourths. Pick the Arugola leaves from the stems. Cut the garlic cloves into fine slices. Heat butter and oil in a frying pan and allow the slices of garlic to fry until crispy. Arrange tomatoes and arugola on a dish. Spread the spring onions, almonds and fried garlic over it and drizzle with dressing.

> **TIP**
> Aromatic vine-ripened tomatoes or plum tomatoes can also be used instead of cherry tomatoes.

Walnut Dressing with Beef Bean Salad

INGREDIENTS: ½ cup dried white beans • 6 tablespoons walnut oil • 2 stalks of thyme • 1 stalk of rosemary • 1 bay leaf • 4 tablespoons balsamic vinegar • salt • sugar • freshly ground pepper • 6 coarsely chopped walnuts • 1 bunch arugola • 2 etrecôte (approximately ½ lb each)

PREPARATION: Soak the white beans overnight in an ample amount of lukewarm water. Then drain and fry for a short time in 1 tablespoons heated cooking oil. Pour water on the beans and add the thyme, rosemary and bay leaf. Then let them boil on low heat until soft. Strain and marinate with 5 tablespoons oil and vinegar. Season with salt, sugar and pepper and decorate with chopped walnuts. Season the etrecôte with salt and pepper and fry on both sides in a grilling pan for 6–8 minutes, or until well-done. Remove from the frying pan, wrap in tin foil and let sit for 5 minutes. Mix the lukewarm bean salad with rinsed, cleaned and well-strained rocket leaves and decorate the dish with them. Take the meat out of the tin foil and cut into thin slices with a sharp knife. Divide the meat into portions onto the prepared plates and drizzle with sauce. Season with pepper.

Yogurt Herb Dressing with Asparagus Rugola Salad

INGREDIENTS: 1 ½ lbs asparagus • salt • sugar • 2 teaspoon highly-concentrated vinegar • 9 oz cherry tomatoes • 1 bunch arugola • 1 cup yogurt • 3 tablespoons olive oil • 4 tablespoons orange juice • some grated orange peels • freshly ground pepper • 1 peeled garlic clove • 2 tablespoons chopped parsley • 2 tablespoons chopped dill • 2 tablespoons chopped chives • 4 slices toasted bread • 2 tablespoons butter • herb salt.

PREPARATION: Peel asparagus and cut into bite-sized pieces. Boil 3 cups salt water with sugar and 1 teaspoon vinegar essence. Cook asparagus until tender. Strain and save water. Wash and dry tomatoes and arugola. Divide fruit and cut off stems. Combine remaining vinegar-essence with yogurt, 2 tablespoons cooking oil, orange juice, orange peels and asparagus cooking water until creamy. Season with salt, pepper, one crushed clove of garlic and herbs. After removing the crust, cube the bread. Heat remaining cooking oil with butter, add bread cubes and cook until crispy. Season with herb salt. Arrange the asparagus, tomatoes, arugola and bread cubes on a dish and pour dressing on top.

Coconut Milk Dressing with Raw Vegetables and Fruits

INGREDIENTS: 1¼ cup sweetened coconut cream • 3½ tablespoons freshly grated ginger • 1 tablespoon curry • 2 teaspoons highly-concentrated vinegar • salt • freshly ground pepper • 2 tablespoons Crème Fraîche • 1 lb white cabbage • 2 bunch radishes • 1 lb cucumbers • 1 lb carrots • 2 beetroots • 2 bunches of cress

PREPARATION: Stir the coconut cream, ginger, curry, vinegar essence, salt, pepper, and Crème Fraîche until it becomes a creamy dressing. Clean and wash the white cabbage and radishes. Grate the cabbage and the radishes into fine strips. Peel the cucumber and cut into small pieces. Clean and peel the carrots and grate them coarsely. Rinse and strain the cress. Arrange all ingredients on a large dish in a decorative fashion and pour the dressing over it.

TIP

Chinese cabbage, white radish, spring onions, small corn cobs and noodles of roast poultry also go splendidly with this original dressing.

Honey Mustard Dressing with Avocado Chicken Salad

INGREDIENTS: ½ lb chicken breast fillet • 1 tablespoon butter • salt • freshly ground pepper • 2 ripe avocados • 4 red onions • 1 pear • ½ head leafy lettuce • 2 tablespoons coarse mustard • 2 tablespoons honey mustard • 1 teaspoon highly-concentrated vinegar • 4 tablespoons germ oil • 4 tablespoons pear juice or instant chicken broth • 10 lemon balm leaves

PREPARATION: Wash the meat and pat dry. Cook in butter for approximately 6 minutes. Season with salt and pepper and let cool. Halve the avocados, core and peel off the skins. Cut the avocado halves into 2 parts. Peel the onions and cut into small

strips. Wash the pears, cut them into quarter pieces, and cut the quarter pieces into small slices. Clean the lettuce and tear in pieces. Place the lettuce, avocados, onions and pear onto plates. Cut the meat into thin slices and put it on the plate. Combine both types of mustard with vinegar, oil, pear juice or chicken broth until creamy to make the dressing. Season with salt and pepper. Cut the balm leaves into strips and stir them into the dressing. Pour the dressing over the salad plate.

Hazelnut Dressing with Corn Salad

INGREDIENTS: 6 tablespoons hazelnut oil • 3½ tablespoons rolled oats • salt • freshly ground pepper • Cayenne pepper • ½–¾ cup lettuce • 1 large carrot • 3 tablespoons balsamic vinegar • 1 tablespoon apple cider vinegar

PREPARATION: Heat 2 tablespoons oil and roast the oats until golden-yellow. Season with salt, pepper and cayenne pepper and let cool. Clean and drain lettuce. Peel the carrot and slice thinly lengthwise. Then cut into match-sized strips. Arrange the lettuce and carrot strips onto plates. Sprinkle roasted oats on top. To make the dressing, combine the remaining oil with the vinegar until creamy. Season to taste with salt, pepper and cayenne pepper and drizzle over the salad.

Olive Lemon Dressing with Bread Salad

TIP
Stale bread is ideal for this simple summer salad because it absorbs the dressing particularly well.

INGREDIENTS: ½ lb olive bread or Ciabatta • 2 peeled tomatoes • 2 peeled red onions • 12 anchovies • 3 oz pitted black olives • 3 hard-boiled eggs • 2 celery stalks with green tops • 2 tablespoons capers• 3 tablespoons chopped parsley • 4 table-spoons lemon juice • 8 tablespoons olive oil • 2 tablespoons white wine vinegar • 3 oz pitted green olives • sugar • freshly ground pepper

PREPARATION: Break the bread into bite-sized pieces. Cut the tomatoes into thin slices and the onions into wafer-thin rings. Chop the anchovies and olives coarsely. Peel the eggs and cut into quarters. Unstring the celery stalks and cut the celery into thin slices at an angle. Mix all ingredients in a bowl. Add the capers and parsley. Mash the green olives and mix with the lemon juice, olive oil and white wine vinegar. Season with salt, sugar and pepper. Pour the dressing over the salad. Pluck the leaves from the celery stalks and sprinkle them on top.

Garlic Dressing with Greek Farmer's Salad

INGREDIENTS: ½ cucumber • 2 large tomatoes • 2 peeled, red onions • ½ Romaine salad • ½ – ¾ cup feta • 12 black pitted olives • 6 tablespoons olive oil • 2 tablespoons rolled oats • 6 peeled garlic cloves • 3 tablespoons lemon juice • 2 tablespoons instant vegetable stock • salt • freshly ground pepper • ½ bunch oregano

PREPARATION: Wash and dry the cucumber and tomatoes. Cut off the tomato stems. Cut the cucumber and tomatoes into slices. Cut the onions into thin rings. Clean the Romaine salad, and pull apart coarsely. Break up the feta with a fork. Place all ingredients onto plates with the olives. Heat 1 tablespoon oil and fry the oats in it until they are golden yellow. Squeeze the garlic through a press. Stir with lemon juice and some broth until creamy. Season the dressing with salt and pepper and drizzle over the salad. Sprinkle everything with fried oats and some of oregano leaves.

Sherry Dressing with Summer Salad

INGREDIENTS: 1 small head iceberg lettuce • 1 head radicchio • 3½ oz Boston lettuce • 1 cucumber • 4 tomatoes • 1 bunch spring onions • 4 tablespoons chives • 4 tablespoons of dry Sherry • 2–3 tablespoons Sherry vinegar • 8 tablespoons olive oil • salt • freshly ground pepper • sugar

PREPARATION: Clean all three types of lettuce. Tear apart the iceberg salad and radicchio. Wash well and drain. Wash the cucumber, wipe dry and slice thinly. Wash the tomatoes, cut off the stems and cut into slices. Clean

the onions and cut only the light and light green parts into thin slices. Mix all salad ingredients in a bowl and sprinkle with chives. Mix the sherry with vinegar and cooking oil until creamy. Season with salt, pepper and some sugar. Pour over the salad and toss.

Maracuja Ginger Dressing with Tomato Banana Salad

INGREDIENTS: 2 bananas • 2 tablespoons lemon juice • 1 lb tomatoes • 3 tablespoons of balsamic vinegar • 2 tablespoons passion fruit juice • 6 tablespoons sunflower oil • 1 teaspoon freshly grated ginger • salt • cayenne pepper • cumin • 1 teaspoon curry • sugar • ½ bunch smooth parsley or cilantro

TIP
If desired, season this unusual salad with a fresh chili husk and sprinkle some roasted cashew nuts on it.

PREPARATION: Peel and slice bananas at an angle. Sprinkle a few drops of lemon juice over them. Put tomatoes in boiling water for a short time, skin, pit and cut into small slices. Mix bananas and tomatoes in a bowl. For dressing, mix vinegar with passion fruit juice and cooking oil until creamy. Season to taste with ginger, salt, cayenne pepper, cumin, 1 teaspoon curry, sugar, parsley or cilantro. Pick cilantro or parsley from stems. Pour dressing over salad and sprinkle herbs on top.

Anchovy Parmesan Dressing with Caesar Salad

INGREDIENTS: 1 large head Romaine lettuce • 2 slices of bread • 2 tablespoons butter • 1 tablespoons sunflower oil • 3 ½ oz bacon • 1 tablespoon anchovy paste • 2 egg yolks • 1 teaspoon hot mustard • 1 peeled garlic clove • 1 tablespoons Worcestershire sauce • 5–6 tablespoons of lemon juice • 3 tablespoons grated parmesan • 1 cup olive oil • salt • freshly ground pepper • cayenne pepper • sugar

PREPARATION: Clean the salad and drain well. Tear into pieces in a bowl. Cut off the bread crusts and cut the bread into small cubes. Heat the butter and cooking oil together and fry the bread in it until it is golden brown. Cut the bacon into fine strips and fry it in the same frying pan until crispy. Drain the croutons and bacon on paper towels. Purée the anchovy paste, egg yolks, mustard, garlic, Worcestershire sauce, lemon juice and parmesan with some oil. Pour remaining cooking oil slowly into it until the dressing is creamy. Pour the dressing over the salad, sprinkle with croutons and bacon.

TIP
This popular American salad is traditionally served in a wooden bowl, which is first rubbed with a garlic clove. Howewer, it is especially good eaten out of a porcelain or glass bowl.

Orange Pepper Dressing with Fennel Salad

INGREDIENTS: 3 oranges • 2 fennel bulbs • 2 red onions • 4 oz Calamata olives • 2–3 tablespoons lime juice • 6 tablespoons grape seed oil • 1 tablespoon pickled green peppercorns • salt • Tabasco sauce • honey • 1 teaspoon crushed red peppercorns

> **TIP**
> For a fine appetizer or a sophisticated party salad mix ½ lb of boiled shrimp or freshwater crayfish into the salad.

PREPARATION: Peel the oranges like apples and cut into sections. Squeeze out the fruits over a bowl. Clean the fennel and grate into fine slices. Add the tender green tops of fennel to the orange juice. Peel the onions and cut into thin rings. Place the orange slices, fennel, onion rings and olives in a large dish. Stir lime juice, oil and mashed peppercorns into the orange juice until creamy. Season with salt, Tabasco sauce and honey. Pour the dressing over the salad and let sit for 30 minutes.

Apple Dressing

TIP
The dressings on this page are suitable for various green salads, raw and steamed vegetables and fruits.

INGREDIENTS: 2 tablespoons peeled sesame • ½ apple • 3 tablespoons lemon juice • 4 tablespoons oil • 1 tablespoon chopped parsley • salt • freshly ground pepper • 1 teaspoon apple juice

PREPARATION: Roast the sesame lightly in a frying pan without fat. Peel the apple, take out the seeds and grate finely. Mix immediately with the sesame and lemon juice. Stir in the oil and parsley and season to taste with salt, pepper and apple juice.

Millet-Vegetable Dressing

INGREDIENTS: 3½ tablespoons millet • 1 cup instant broth mix • 1 carrot • 2 oz mushrooms • 2 oz leaf spinach • 1 peeled garlic clove • 4 tablespoons oil • 3 tablespoons lemon juice • salt • freshly ground pepper • freshly grated nutmeg

PREPARATION: Wash the millet and cook in broth 20 minutes. Let drain in a strainer and catch the broth. Clean the vegetables, dice coarsely and let simmer for 8 minutes with the garlic in some germ oil and the broth. Strain the vegetables, pureé with a hand mixer and stir in the millet, remaining oil and lemon juice. Season to taste with salt, pepper and nutmeg.

Wheat Herb Dressing

INGREDIENTS: 3 ½ tablespoons wheat grains • 1 teaspoon instant broth mix • 3 ½ oz yogurt • 2 tablespoons lemon juice • 4 tablespoons oil • 4 tablespoons mixed chopped herbs • salt • freshly ground pepper • cayenne pepper • sugar

PREPARATION: Soak the wheat grains overnight in a lot of cold water. Stir in the broth and let simmer for 40 minutes. Strain the wheat and let drain. Stir the yogurt with oil, lemon juice, wheat grains and chopped herbs until creamy. Season to taste with salt, pepper and sugar.

French Dressing

INGREDIENTS: 1 tablespoon tomato ketchup • 1 teaspoon Dijon mustard • 2 tablespoons brandy • 2 tablespoons mayonnaise • 2 tablespoons lemon juice • 1 chopped shallot • 2 tablespoons oil • salt • freshly ground pepper • cayenne pepper

PREPARATION: Stir the tomato ketchup with mustard, brandy and mayonnaise until smooth. Stir in lemon juice, shallot and oil. Season to taste with salt, pepper and some cayenne pepper.

TIP
This sauce tastes particularly good with shrimp and endive salad.

Pecan Dressing with Apple Cheese Salad

TIP
You can also use tasty pears for this sweet-and-sour salad.

INGREDIENTS: 2 tablespoons mayonnaise • 5 tablespoons sour cream • 4 tablespoons walnut oil • 4 tablespoons apple vinegar • 2 tablespoons apple juice • 1 teaspoon apple sauce • 10 black peppercorns • 7 tablespoons pecans • salt • curry • ¾ lb Swiss cheese • 1lb red apples, peeled • 1 stalk of dill

PREPARATION: Mix the mayonnaise with the sour cream, oil, vinegar, apple juice and apple sauce until creamy. Crush the peppercorns in a mortar. Chop the nuts very coarsely. Add both to the dressing and let sit for a short

time. Then season to taste with salt and some curry. Cut the cheese into small cubes without the rind. Wash the apples, cut into quarters, remove the seeds and dice. Mix with the dressing and let sit 30 minutes. Then garnish with some dill.

Carrot Orange Dressing with Cauliflower Salad

INGREDIENTS: 1 small cauliflower • salt • 1 cup milk • freshly grated nutmeg • 6 scallops without shells • 2 tablespoons butter • freshly ground pepper • 2 table-spoons poppy seeds • 2 blood oranges • 2 tablespoons lime juice • 3 tablespoons poppy seed oil • cayenne pepper • some chervil

PREPARATION: Divide the cauliflower into small flowerets. Bring to a boil 1 cup salt water with milk and a lot of nutmeg. Cook the cauliflower flowerets in it until soft. Strain and let drain. Wash the scallop, dab dry and fry in hot fat on each side for 30 seconds. Add salt and pepper. Cut the lukewarm scallops into strips and mix with the cauliflower flowerets. Fry the poppy seeds in a frying pan without fat. Slice a blood orange and squeeze out the others. Add the orange slices to the cauliflower. Stir the orange juice with poppy seeds, lime juice and oil until creamy. Season with salt, pepper, and cayenne pepper and pour over the salad. Let stand for 30 minutes and garnish with chervil.

TIP
Half of the cauliflower can be replaced by the same amount of broccoli. Neither vegetable should be overcooked.

Pumpkin Dressing with Potato Salad

INGREDIENTS: 1 ½ lb boiling potatoes • ½ cup hot instant meat broth • 1 small apple • 1 red onion • 1 small pickle • 4 thick radishes • 3 ½ tablespoons radish sprouts • 2 tablespoons capers • 1 chopped red chili pepper • 6 tablespoons pumpkin seeds • 5 tablespoons pumpkin oil • salt • cayenne pepper • 6 tablespoons lemon juice • ½ cup yogurt • juice from 1 mandarin orange • 1 teaspoon grated horseradish • honey • 4 tablespoons chopped chives

PREPARATION: Cook potatoes for 25 minutes, drain, peel and slice. Pour the hot broth over mixture immediately. Wash, dry and core apples. Then cut into thin slices. Peel the onion and cut into thin half-rings. Dice the pickle coarsely. Grate clean radishes. Wash sprouts. Drain the cooled potatoes and mix with apple slices, onions, diced gherkin, radishes, sprouts, capers and chili. Roast pumpkin seeds in frying pan without fat. Mix with one tablespoon oil, salt, and some cayenne pepper. Stir remaining oil with lemon juice, yogurt, mandarin juice and horseradish until creamy. Season with salt, cayenne pepper and some honey. Mix dressing with salad first, then fold in pumpkin seeds. Let sit for 30 minutes and sprinkle with chives.

> **TIP**
> This potato salad tastes particularly good if the lukewarm pieces of potato are immediately covered with a lot of hot meat broth and left to sit overnight.

Apricot Mint Dressing with Rice Salad

INGREDIENTS: 7 tablespoons brown rice • 4 cups instant chicken broth • 2 bay leaves • 1 teaspoon curry • 4 dried apricots • ½ lb chicken breast fillet • 1 tablespoon butter • 1 tablespoon cumin seeds • salt • freshly ground pepper • 4 tablespoons apricot nectar • 4 tablespoons oil • ½ cup yogurt • 5–6 tablespoons lemon juice • 1 tablespoon soy sauce • 1 teaspoon freshly chopped ginger • 2 chopped spring onions • 1 tablespoon sesame seeds • 8 peppermint leaves • 1 ripe apricot

PREPARATION: Wash the rice, bring the broth with bay leaves and curry. Let rice cook slowly for 40–45 minutes. Cook apricots slowly with the rice during the last 10 minutes. Drain the rice. Cut apricots into small pieces and mix in a bowl with the rice. Wash meat, dry, and fry in hot fat with cumin seeds on each side for 3–4 minutes. Salt and pepper. For dressing, stir the nectar with oil, yogurt, lemon juice and soy sauce until creamy. Mix with ginger, spring onions, and sesame and season with salt and pepper. Cut mint leaves into strips and add to dressing. Dice cooled meat and mix with rice. Pour dressing over it and let sit for 30 minutes. Wash apricot, wipe dry, cut into quarters, core and then cut into strips to garnish the salad.

Salsas, Chutneys & Dips

On the following pages, you will find a series of delicate tidbits from the international sauce kitchen. Salsas, chutneys, relishes, raita and dips enrich meat, fish, and poultry dishes and curries. Most of them consist of fresh ingredients. They are sometimes hot, sometimes mild. Salsas originated in Mexico. Chutneys, consisting mainly of fruit, or relishes, made from vegetables, come from India. The former are made from fruit and the latter are mostly made of vegetables. The refreshing raitas of Indian origin have a yogurt base and are added to hot and spicy dishes. Dips are compact sauces in which chips, bread sticks, vegetables and potato sticks are dipped.

Guacamole

INGREDIENTS: 2–3 ripe avocados • 2 limes • 2 peeled cloves of garlic • 2 tomatoes • 2 chopped red chili peppers • 1 tablespoon chopped cilantro • salt • freshly ground pepper

PREPARATION: Halve the avocados lengthwise. Remove the pits and peel the fruits. Afterwards, dice coarsely. Wash the limes in hot water, dry and grate one of the peels into the avocados. Squeeze out the pulp as well as the lime juice and pour into the avocados. Mash the garlic with a press and stir into the mix. Purée everything but not too finely with the hand mixer. Skin the tomatoes, core and dice very finely. Stir the diced tomatoes, chili and cilantro into the guacamole and season with salt and pepper.

TIP

If the avocados are very ripe, then their peels will be easy to remove. Wrap solid fruits in newspaper and let ripen for a few days.

Cranberry Salsa with Roast Beef

INGREDIENTS: 2 lbs roast beef • 2 teaspoons Thomy Sonne & Olive oil • 1 prepackaged seasoning mixture • ½ cup red wine • 1 cup sugar • 1 piece lemon peel • ½ lb cranberries • 3 tablespoons salsa • 1 orange • 2 small packets of instant delicatessen sauce for frying • 2 peeled garlic cloves • 1 teaspoon Worcestershire sauce

> **TIP**
> Instead of fresh cranberries, preserved cranberries (jam) can also be used. In the latter case, the thickening step can be omitted.

PREPARATION: Wash the meat, dab dry, and cut the fatty side into diamond shapes. Preheat the oven to 475°F. Cook the roast beef on a greased broiler pan for 15 minutes. Reduce the temperature to 350°F and cook for an additional 20–40 minutes until medium pink. Mix ½ cup water with red wine, sugar, and lemon peel. Add the cranberries and cook slowly. Let the cranberries drain in a strainer and catch the juice. Mix the cranberries with salsa. Squeeze out the orange and fill with cranberry juice up to 2 cups. Stir in the sauce powder and bring to a boil. Squeeze the garlic into it. Add the frying juice from the juice pan and season to taste with Worcestershire sauce.

Mango Tomato Salsa

INGREDIENTS: 1 can pizza tomatoes • 1 ripe mango • 2 spring onions • 2 peeled garlic cloves • 2 chopped green chili peppers • 4 tablespoons lime juice • salt • freshly ground pepper • 1 tablespoon honey • 6 peppermint leaves in strips

PREPARATION: Cook the tomatoes until they are thick and creamy. Dice the mango finely. Also chop the spring onions very finely. Mix both with the tomato sauce. Squeeze the garlic into it. Add the chili and lime juice and season the salsa to taste with salt, pepper, honey and mint.

Red Pepper Lime Salsa

INGREDIENTS: 2 red peppers • 3 limes • 3 chopped red onions • 2 chopped green chili husks • 1 tablespoon tomato ketchup • 2 tablespoons Chinese sweet-and-sour chili sauce • 10 coriander seeds • 10 Sezchuan peppercorns • ½ teaspoon cumin seeds • salt • sugar

PREPARATION: Peel the peppers and chop into medium-fine pieces. Grate one lime peel into the peppers. Peel the limes and cut into sections. Squeeze out the remainder of the fruits over the peppers. Add the lime pieces, onions, chili, ketchup and chili sauce to the paprika. Grate the seasoning peppers and mix into the salsa. Season to taste with salt and pepper.

Macadamia Salsa with Turkey Saté

INGREDIENTS: 1¼ lb turkey breast • 1 lime • 5 tablespoons soy sauce • 2 tablespoons dark sesame oil • ½ cup of chopped macadamia nuts • 4 tablespoons sunflower oil • 2 chopped shallots • 1 chopped garlic clove • 2 choppe green chili peppers • 3 tablespoons brown sugar • 3 table-spoons rice vinegar • 1½ cups coconut milk • salt • 4 stalks lemon grass • 7 tablespoons garlic butter • ½ bunch cilantro

PREPARATION: Wash and dab dry meat and lime. Cut meat into finger-wide strips. Grate lime peel and squeeze out the fruit. Then mix half the juice and the peel with 2 tablespoons soy sauce and sesame oil and marinate meat for 30 minutes. Roast the macadamia nuts in 2 tablespoons oil. Stir in the shallots, garlic, chili, and sugar and simmer for 1 minute. Stir in the remaining lime peel, juice, vinegar, remaining soy sauce, and coconut milk and thicken until creamy for 8–10 minutes. Season to taste with salt. Cut the lemon grass to a point and thread the marinated meat onto spits. Fry 1 minute in remaining oil. Cut garlic butter into slices and add to spits and fry 3–4 minutes until finished. Sprinkle cilantro over lukewarm salsa and serve with saté skewers.

Zucchini Corn Salsa

INGREDIENTS: 1 can corn • 4 tablespoons olive oil • ½–¾ lb zucchini • 1 bunch spring onions • 2 peeled garlic cloves • 2 chopped red chili peppers • 1 lime • salt • 8 chopped peppermint leaves

PREPARATION: Drain the corn and dry well. Heat some oil and fry the corn seeds until golden brown. Grate the zucchini coarsely. Mix with the remaining oil and corn. Clean the spring onions and cut very finely. Add to the vegetables, squeeze the garlic in, stir in the chili, wash, pat dry and peel the lime. Squeeze out the fruit. Add to the sauce and season to taste with salt and mint.

Chili Salsa

INGREDIENTS: 5 dried chili peppers • 3 mild red chili peppers • 2 green chili peppers • 4 skinned tomatoes • juice and one lemon peel • salt • sugar • cumin powder • 2 tablespoons chopped cilantro

PREPARATION: Soak dried chili peppers for 30 minutes in warm water. Let drain, cut off the husks and dice the pods. Chop the fresh chili husks and tomatoes finely. Mix everything with lemon juice and lemon peel. Season to taste with the spices and cilantro

Tomato Ginger Salsa with Meat Skewers

INGREDIENTS: ¼ lb tomatoes • 3½ tablespoons ginger • 2 red chili husks • 1 teablespoon salsa • 1 blood orange • 1 lime • 1 peeled chopped garlic clove • 1 white peeled onion • salt • sugar • ½ lb neck cutlet • ½ lb rump steak • freshly ground pepper • 5 oz smoked ham • 3 table-spoons olive oil

PREPARATION: Put the tomatoes in boiling water for a short time. Cut off the stems, skin and core. Chop the tomatoes coarsely. Peel the ginger and grate finely. Chop the chili finely and mix it with the ginger, salsa and tomatoes. Peel the orange like an apple and separate the sections. Squeeze the remaining fruit over the tomatoes. Wash the lime, rub dry and grate the peel into the tomatoes. Squeeze out the fruit and combine with the garlic, orange sections and tomatoes. Grate the onion finely into it and season to taste with salt and sugar. Wash the meat, dab dry and cut into large cubes. Season with salt and pepper. Slice the ham lengthwise and wrap every piece of meat with ham. Put the meat cubes onto 4 skewers and fry in hot cooking oil in a grilling pan until golden brown all over.

Apple Chutney

INGREDIENTS: 2 lbs apples • 5 oz onions • 2 tablespoons ginger • ½ cup raisins • 1 tablespoon mustard seeds • 5 tablespoons highly concentrated vinegar • 1 lb brown crystallized sugar • salt • cayenne pepper

PREPARATION: Cut the apple into quarters, peel, core and cut into thin slices. Peel the onions and ginger and dice finely. Add all ingredients with the raisins, mustard seeds, highly-concentrated vinegar, 1 cup of water, crystallized sugar, approximately one heaping teaspoon salt and cayenne pepper into a large pot and mix. Simmer until

slightly thick while stirring without a cover for 40-50 minutes. Fill twist-off glasses with the hot chutney.

Apricot Banana Chutney

INGREDIENTS: 2 lbs juicy apricots • ¾ lb of peeled bananas • 2 lb of sugar • ½ cup of Corinth • 5 oz green bell peppers, chopped • 7 tablespoons highly-concentrated vinegar • 1 teaspoon black peppercorns • cayenne pepper • ground allspice • ground cardamom • 1 teaspoon grated orange peel

TIP
Use mangos instead of apricots for this chutney.

DIRECTIONS FOR PREPARATION: Wash the apricots and rub dry. Halve the fruits, remove the seeds and dice. Halve the bananas as well. Mix the fruit with sugar and let sit for 30 minutes. Let the mix simmer while stirring often for 1 hour. Stir in the Corinth, peppers and vinegar. Crush the peppercorns in a mortar and add some Cayenne pepper, cloves, cardamom and orange peel and let the chutney simmer without a cover for an additional 30 minutes. Fill twist-off glasses with hot chutney.

Currant Chutney

TIP
This chutney has a particularly spicy taste if approximately half of it consists of black currants.

INGREDIENTS: 2 lbs red currants • 2 lbs sugar • 1 untreated lemon • 2 un-treated oranges • 1 cup red wine • 2 tablespoons mustard powder • 6 tablespoons highly-concentrated vinegar

PREPARATION: Wash the currants and drain well. Pluck the berries from the stems and mix with sugar. Let the juice sit for 30 minutes. Wash and dry the citrus fruits. Peel all the fruits with a peeler into strips. Squeeze out the fruits. Let the peeled strips cook in the red wine for 5 minutes. Add the currants, citrus juices, and mustard powder to the wine and cook until the berries burst. Stir in the highly-concentrated vinegar and let simmer without a cover for an additional 15 minutes. Then pour hot into twist-off glasses.

Pineapple Chutney

INGREDIENTS: 1 ripe pineapple • 1 white onion • 1 lime
• sugar • salt • 1 teaspoon dark mustard seeds • ½ teaspoon
coriander seeds • 1 teaspoon olive oil • ½ teaspoon starch

PREPARATION: Cut pineapples lengthwise into quarters.
Peel, core and chop fruit coarsely. Peel and cube onions
finely. Add to pineapples. Wash and dry lime. Squeeze lime
juice into chutney and add lime peelings. Purée uncovered
10–20 minutes, or until thick and creamy. Season with salt
and sugar. Roast seasoning seeds in cooking oil, crush and
add to chutney. Stir in cold water until smooth. Boil chutney and let cool.

Cilantro Parsley Chutney

INGREDIENTS: 4 tablespoons dried coconut • 2 chopped
red chili peppers • 4 chopped cloves of garlic • 3 tablespoons lime juice • 2 ½ tablespoons cilantro • 2 ½ tablespoons parsley leaves • salt • sugar

PREPARATION: Fry coconut lightly in a pan without fat. Mix
with chili, garlic and lime juice. Add roughly chopped
herbs. Season with salt and sugar.

Rhubarb Almond Chutney

TIP
In India, the house wife makes fresh chutney daily. It is served with all rice, meat and fish dishes.

INGREDIENTS: 2 ½ lbs rhubarb • 1 lb of apples • 1 lb brown sugar • 10 tablespoons highly-concentrated vinegar • 1 teaspoon grated ginger • 3 tablespoons almond bits • 7 tablespoons pitless prunes • 7 tablespoons raisins • 2 chopped red chili peppers • 1 teablespoon mustard seeds

PREPARATION: Clean the rhubarb, wash and let drain well. Cut the apples into quarters, peel and core. Cut the rhubarb and apples into small pieces.

Cook them with sugar, highly-concentrated vinegar and ½ cup water without a cover until mixture becomes moderately thick. Add the ginger, pieces of almonds, the small cut prunes, raisins, chili and mustard seeds to it and let cook slowly without a cover for 1 additional hour. Fill twist-off glasses with the hot chutney.

Tomato Cucumber Onion Relish

INGREDIENTS: ½ lb tomatoes • ½ lb cored cucumbers • ½ lb red onions • 1 peeled garlic clove • 2 chopped green chili peppers • 3 tablespoons lime juice • 1 teaspoon olive oil • salt • sugar • 4 tablespoons coarsely chopped cilantro

PREPARATION: Skin the tomatoes, core and cut into very small pieces. Peel and chop the cucumber into pieces of the same size. Peel and dice the onions, but not too finely. Chop the garlic finely. Mix the tomatoes, cucumber, onions, garlic, chili, lime juice and oil. Season to taste with salt, sugar and cilantro.

TIP
Like fresh chutney, a relish should sit at least 30 minutes in the refrigerator.

Sweet and Sour Relish

INGREDIENTS: 5 oz pickles • 5 oz of pickled mustard gherkins • 3 ½ oz pickled pearl onions • 5 oz mustard seed fruits • 1 tablespoon hot mustard • 1 teablespoon olive oil • 2 tablespoons chopped parsley • Cayenne pepper

Mix chopped, solid ingredients with mustard, oil and parsley. Season to taste with cayenne pepper.

Celery Apple Relish

INGREDIENTS: 2 lbs celery stalks • 2 lbs slightly sour apples • ½ lb carrots • 1 lb onions • 1 cup apple juice • ½ lb brown sugar • 1 cup crystallized sugar • 1 cup raisins • 10 cloves • 1 teablespoon mustard seeds • 2 bay leaves • 5 tablespoons highly-concentrated vinegar • salt • freshly ground pepper

TIP
Cooked chutneys and relishes stay edible in twist-off jars in the refrigerator for 2–3 months. Fresh chutneys and relishes should be consumed in 1–2 days.

PREPARATION: Clean and unstring the celery. Cut the apples into quarters, peel and core. Cut the celery and apples into fine slices. Peel the carrots and onions and dice very finely. Heat up the apple juice with sugars. Add the vegetables, fruit, raisins and spices and cook in an open pot for 1 hour, or until slightly thick. Add the highly-concentrated vinegar after 30 minutes. Season the relish to taste with salt and pepper. Fill twist-off jars with hot relish.

Onion Cranberry Relish

INGREDIENTS: 2 lbs red onions • 2 lbs cranberries • 1 lb brown sugar • 2 chopped • red chili peppers • 5 tablespoons highly-concentrated vinegar • 1 cup red wine • 7 tablespoons Crème de Cassis • 1 tablespoon salt

PREPARATION: Peel the onions and cube finely. Clean the cranberries, wash and drain well. Mix the onions, cranberries, sugar and chili. Let everything sit for 30 minutes. Stir in the remaining ingredients and cook in an open pot for 45–60 minutes until mixture becomes thick. Put the hot relish into twist-off jars.

> **TIP**
> The glasses and covers for relishes and chutneys must be carefully cleaned and rinsed in hot water before the hot ingredients can be poured into them.

Horseradish Apple Relish

INGREDIENTS: 3 ½ inch stalk horseradish • 1 sour apple • 4 spring onions • 4 tablespoons lemon juice • 1 tablespoon honey • 1 teaspoon Worcestershire sauce • 4 tablespoons mayonnaise • salt • freshly ground pepper • cayenne pepper

PREPARATION: Peel and finely grate the horseradish stalk. Cut the apple into quarters, peel and core. Grate the apple quarters coarsely into the horseradish. Clean the spring onions and cut into very fine pieces. Stir into the horseradish-apple mix. Mix lemon juice, honey, Worcestershire sauce and mayonnaise until smooth. Add solid ingredients and mix. Season to taste with salt, pepper and cayenne pepper.

Zucchini Relish

INGREDIENTS: 2 lbs zucchini • 2 lbs onions
• ½ cup olive oil • 3 peeled garlic cloves
• 3 red chili peppers • ½ cup dry sherry
• 5 tablespoons highly-concentrated vinegar
• salt • freshly ground pepper • 4 tablespoons sugar

PREPARATION: Clean the zucchini, wash, rub dry
and dice. Peel the onions and also dice. Let
both simmer in heated cooking oil until juicy
and stir 20 minutes. Add mashed garlic (using
a press) to the mix. Chop the chili peppers finely, adding the sherry
and highly concen-
trated vinegar to the
mix. Cook all ingre-
dients without a co-
ver in a pot for an
additional 30 min-
utes until thick. Sea-
son to taste with salt,
pepper, and sugar.
Pour the hot relish
into twist-off jars.

> **TIP**
> This striking relish can also be pre-
> pared with the same amount of
> Hokkaido pumpkin instead of
> zucchini. The pumpkin relish is
> then additionally seasoned with
> some freshly grated ginger and
> 1 pinch cinnamon.

Cucumber Raita with Vegetable Skewers

INGREDIENTS: 8 shallots • ¾ lb broccoli • salt • 8 mushrooms • 3 tablespoons olive oil • 1 red bell pepper • 1 yellow bell pepper • freshly ground pepper • cayenne pepper • ½ teaspoon cumin seeds • ½ teaspoon coriander seeds • 1 ¾ cups of yogurt • 1 peeled garlic clove • 1 chopped green chili pepper • ½ cucumber • 2 tablespoons chopped cilantro • salt

PREPARATION: Cook unpeeled shallots slowly in water for 10 minutes. Then drain and peel. Divide broccoli into florets, cook slowly and drain well. Clean and fry mushrooms in cooking oil. Clean bell peppers an cut into bite-size pieces. Arrange vegetables on long skewers and spread cooking oil over them. Salt and pepper. Fry in grilling pan 10–15 minutes. Add cayenne pepper. Heat a little cooking oil in frying pan and roast spice seds until fragrant. Cool and crush seeds in mortar. Mix seasoning powder with yoghurt, mashed garlic and chili. Peel, core and coarsely grate cucumber into yoghurt. Season with cilantro, salt and pepper.

Avocado Raita with Chicken Legs

INGREDIENTS: 4 chicken legs • 4 tablespoons olive oil • 2 tablespoons sherry • 1 tablespoon Chinese sweet-and-sour chili sauce • 1 teaspoon curry powder • 1 teaspoon cayenne pepper • 1 teaspoon cumin • 1 chopped clove of garlic • 1¾ cups yogurt • 1 lime • 1 chopped • 1 green chili husk • 2 chopped spring onions • 1 ripe avocado • 2 tablespoons chopped cilantro or cress • salt • freshly ground pepper • sugar • 3 tablespoons cashews

PREPARATION: Wash and dab dry the chicken legs. Mix 2 tablespoons oil with sherry, chili sauce, curry, cayenne pepper, cumin and garlic. Spread it on the legs and let sit for at least 3 hours. Heat the remaining oil in a broiler pan and cook the legs for 30–35 minutes. Mix the yogurt with lime juice and peel, chili and spring onions. Peel the avocado, core and dice finely. Add to the yogurt with the herbs. Season everything to taste with salt, pepper and sugar. Roast the cashews in a frying pan without fat and sprinkle over the raita. Sprinkle salt and pepper on the chicken legs before serving.

Tomato Ketchup

INGREDIENTS: 4 lbs very ripe tomatoes • ½ lb onions
• 2 bay leaves • 3 cloves • 10 allspice berries • ½ cup
apple vinegar • ½ cinnamon stick • 5 tablespoons sugar
• 3 teaspoons salt

PREPARATION: Wash and stem tomatoes. Peel onions. Chop
both coarsely and simmer uncov-
ered with the other ingredients for
40 minutes. Strain. Cook 25–35
minutes more. Bottle whille hot.

> **TIP**
> Store ketchup and mustard
> in a cool place and consume
> shortly after opening.

Coarse Ground Mustard

INGREDIENTS: 2 tablespoons black mustard seeds • 2 tablespoons yellow mustard seeds • 3 tablespoons mustard
powder • ½ teaspoon salt • ½ teaspoon sugar • ½ teaspoon
grated orange peel • apple cider or white wine

PREPARATION: Boil mustard seeds until soft. Drain and
grind coarsely in a mortar. Stir mustard powder into a paste
with a little cold water and mix with mustard seeds, salt,
sugar and orange peel. Add vinegar or wine to desired consistency.

Orange Dip

INGREDIENTS: ½ cup of cream • ½ teaspoon grated orange peel • 3 tablespoons orange juice • or orange liquor • 1 teaspoon orange mustard • ginger powder • salt • freshly ground white pepper

PREPARATION: Whip the cream until firm. Stir orange peel, orange juice or liquor and mustard together until smooth. Add to the cream and season to taste with ginger, salt and pepper.

Gorgonzola Dip

INGREDIENTS: 1 spring onion • 4 walnuts • ½ cup gorgonzola • 3 tablespoons yogurt salad crème • ½ cup cream cheese (20% fat)

PREPARATION: Clean the spring onions and chop the light part very finely. Chop the walnuts. Mash the gorgonzola with a fork and mix with onions, walnuts, salad cream, and cream cheese.

Tomato Pepper Dip

INGREDIENTS: 1 lb tomatoes • 1 red bell pepper • 2 red chili peppers • 4 spring onions • 2 peeled garlic cloves • 2 tablespoons capers • some grated lemon peel • 1 tablespoon olive oil • salt • freshly ground pepper • cayenne pepper • 2 tablespoons parsley

PREPARATION: Put the tomatoes in boiling water for a short time, skin, core and be careful not to chop too finely. Strain the tomato seeds. Peel the bell pepper with a fine peeler, halve, clean, and dice. Cook slowly in a small amount of water for 10 minutes, drain, and mix with the tomatoes. Chop the chili pepper finely. Clean the spring onions and dice only the light part finely. Squeeze the garlic through a press. Chop the capers finely. Mix the tomato liquid, chili, onions, and garlic with the tomatoes. Season to taste with lemon peel, olive oil, salt, pepper, cayenne pepper and parsley.

Arugola Dip

INGREDIENTS: 1 bunch arugola • 1 peeled garlic clove • 1 red onion • 4 tablespoons pine nuts • ½ lb full-fat herb cheese • 2–3 tablespoons yogurt or milk • 2 tablespoons lemon juice • salt • cayenne pepper

PREPARATION: Clean the arugola, wash and let drain well. Chop the leaves. Press the garlic into the leaves with a garlic press. Peel and cube the onions finely. Roast the pine nuts in a frying pan without fat and chop coarsely. Toss onions and pine nuts with arugola, fresh cheese, yogurt or milk and lemon juice until smooth. Season with salt and cayenne pepper.

Cilantro Mayonnaise Dip

INGREDIENTS: 7 tablespoons delicatessen mayonnaise • 4 tablespoons sour cream • 1 teaspoon lemon juice • 1 peeled garlic clove • 6 tablespoons chopped cilantro • salt • freshly ground pepper

PREPARATION: Stir the mayonnaise with cream and lemon juice until smooth. Squeeze the garlic into it. Add the cilantro, some salt, and pepper.

Almond Dip with Dried Tomatoes

INGREDIENTS: 7 tablespoons almonds (whole and peeled) • 7 tablespoons dried tomatoes in cooking oil • 4 tablespoons tomato juice or instant vegetable stock • 3½ teaspoon black olives without seeds • 2 tablespoons olive oil • 1 bunch basil • 1 tablespoon lemon juice • 2 peeled • chopped garlic cloves • salt • freshly ground pepper

PREPARATION: Roast the almonds in a frying pan without fat until golden yellow. Let cool. Chop the roasted almonds into moderately sized pieces. Let the tomatoes drain and also chop them into moderately sized pieces. Mix the almonds and tomatoes together with tomato juice or broth. Chop the olives coarsely. Add oil, lemon juice and garlic to the almond-tomato mixture. Wash and dry the basil. Pluck the leaves from the stalks and chop. Add to the dip along with salt and pepper. Stir everything together well.

Nut Dip with Red Beet Slices

INGREDIENTS: 1 lb red beets • 2 eggs • salt • freshly ground pepper • 1 cup rolled oats • frying fat • 4 tablespoons hazelnuts • 1 teablespoon hazelnut purée • 1¼ cups yogurt • grated orange peel • lemon juice • honey

PREPARATION: Clean the red beets and cook slowly in an ample amount of water for 50–60 minutes. Peel the cooled vegetables and cut into thick slices. Mix the egg with some salt and pepper and add a bit of water to it on a plate. Dip the vegetable slices in the egg and press them into the oats. Heat the fat in a frying pan. Fry the breaded red beet slices until golden yellow on both sides. Absorb the fat from them on kitchen paper towels. For the dip, roast the hazelnuts in a frying pan without fat and chop coarsely. Stir into hazelnut purée and yogurt. Season the dip to taste with salt, pepper, orange peel, lemon juice and honey.

Smoked Salmon Dip with Potatoes

INGREDIENTS: 1 cup cream cheese (20% fat) • 1 teaspoon oil • 3–4 tablespoons milk • 1 pouch salad dressing for plain onion herb sause • 4 oz smoked salmon • ½ bunch dill

PREPARATION: Stir the cream cheese with oil and milk until creamy. Add the salad dressing. Dice the smoked salmon into very small pieces. Wash the dill, remove it from the stems. Mix the salmon and dill with the cream cheese.

Cream Cheese Pepper Dip with Potatoes

INGREDIENTS: ½ red bell pepper • ½ lb cream cheese • 2 tablespoons herbs for sprinkling • 1 green chili pepper • cayenne pepper

PREPARATION: Peel the bell pepper with a paring tool and dice finely. Mix the cream cheese with herbs and bell pepper. Dice the chili pepper finely and add to the cream cheese. Season to taste with cayenne pepper.

Pea Bacon Dip

INGREDIENTS: ¾ lb frozen peas • salt • ground nutmeg •
2 oz bacon • 2 tablespoons olive oil • 2 peeled cloves of
garlic • 2 spring onions • 2 tablespoons chopped chervil
• 2 chopped peppermint leaves • pepper

PREPARATION: Cook the peas in salt water with nutmeg for
8 minutes. Drain and save water. Cube bacon and fry until
crispy. Absorb the extra fat with paper towels. Crush garlic. Chop spring onions. Purée peas with some of saved
cooking water. Mix pea purée with bacon, garlic, spring
onions, cooking oil and herbs. Add salt and pepper.

Black Bean Dip

INGREDIENTS: 1 cup cooked black beans • approximately
1 cup bean cooking water • 2 red chopped onions •
2 chopped cloves of garlic • 4 tablespoons tahini (sesame
paste) • 1 red chopped chili pepper • 1 chopped green
chili pepper • 4 tablespoons olive oil • cumin • coriander
• salt • lemon juice

PREPARATION: Purée the beans with cooking water. Stir in
other ingredients and season.

Curry Apricot Dip

INGREDIENTS: 5 oz dried apricots • 1 cup apricot nectar • 4 tablespoons lemon juice • ½ teaspoon freshly chopped ginger • ½ cup Crème Fraîche • ½ cup yogurt • 4 tablespoons chopped pistachios • 1 teaspoon of curry powder • salt • cayenne pepper

PREPARATION: Cook the apricots slowly for 15 minutes in apricot nectar. Strain and drain well. Save the juice. Cube the apricots finely and mix with nectar, lemon juice, ginger and Crème Fraîche. Season the dip to taste with curry, salt, and cayenne pepper.

Eggplant Garlic Dip

INGREDIENTS: 1 lb eggplants • 6–8 tablespoons olive oil • 4 peeled garlic cloves • 2 tablespoons chopped cilantro • salt • freshly ground pepper • cayenne pepper • lemon juice

PREPARATION: Halve the eggplants and spread some cooking oil over the surface, then wrap loosely in aluminum foil. Cook slowly in the oven at 350°F for 45–55 minutes. Remove the soft flesh of the fruit and purée. Add mashed garlic. Stir in the cooking oil and cilantro and season to taste with salt, pepper, cayenne pepper and lemon juice.

Olive Dip

INGREDIENTS: ¾ cup pitted black olives • ¾ cup pitted green olives • 2 peeled garlic cloves • 2 anchovy filets • 2 tablespoons Dijon mustard • 2 tablespoons fresh thyme leaves • ½ cup olive oil • some grated orange peel • 4 tablespoons lime juice • salt • freshly ground pepper • cayenne pepper

---

TIP

This dip gets a fruity taste if 3½ tablespoons finely chopped dried tomatoes are stirred into it.

PREPARATION: Chop the olives finely. Add crushed garlic. Rinse, dab dry and chop the anchovy filets very finely. Add mustard, thyme leaves, cooking oil, orange peel and lime juice to the olives and mix well. Season the dip to taste with salt, pepper and Cayenne pepper.

Sweet Sauces

Nothing pleases people more than something sweet after a good meal. Dessert sauces, whether plain vanilla sauce, gently melting chocolate, solid marzipan sauce or a sugar sweet caramel, accompany soufflés and puddings, fruits or pastries beautifully. In our last chapter, you will encounter exquisite sauces such as Whiskey Cream Sauce, Ice Cream Sauce or fruity Grappa Grapes Sauce for Baked Camembert.

English Creme for Rum-Dipped-Fruits

INGREDIENTS: 6 egg yolks • 5 tablespoons sugar • 2 vanilla beans • 2 cups milk • 1 pinch salt • 12–15 tablespoons rum dipped fruits • 4 pastry rolls

PREPARATION: Stir the egg yolks with sugar until very foamy. Cut the vanilla beans lengthwise and scrape out the pulp. Combine the vanilla pulp with the vanilla husks, bring to a boil in the milk and let sit for 15 minutes. Remove the husks and mix the hot milk with some salt and the egg yolk mixture. Heat at medium temperature on the stove, but don't boil until the

TIP
Pour the hot milk in a thin stream into the egg-sugar-mixture.

cream is bound. Divide the rum dipped fruit into glass bowls and put the lukewarm English Creme over them. Garnish each bowl with a piece of pastry.

Zabaione with Strawberry Sparkling Wine Jelly

INGREDIENTS: 7 slices gelatin • 1 cup sugar • 2 limes • 1 lb strawberries • 2 cups Rosé sparkling wine • 4 egg yolks • 2 egg whites • 1 orange • 1 bag of orange-flavored baking agent • ½ cup of orange liquor • 1 bag chopped pistachio nuts • 1 bag white Chocolate Flakes

PREPARATION: Soak the gelatin in cold water for 10 minutes. Boil ½ cup sugar with 5 tablespoons water to a light color syrup. Wash and dry 1 lime. Grate the peel and add gratings to syrup. Squeeze out the fruit juice and mix with the syrup. Melt jelly in the warm syrup while stirring. Then strain it through a fine strainer. Clean strawberries, wash them and cut in small pieces. Mix the fruits with sparkling wine and syrup and pour into glasses. Place glasses in the refrigerator to solidify for 3-4 hours. To prepare the Zabaione, whisk egg yolks with egg whites, the remaining sugar, orange juice, orange-flavored baking agent and liquor in a water bath until foamy. Garnish the jelly with pistachio nuts and chocolate flakes.

Whiskey Cream Sauce with Stewed Cherry

INGREDIENTS: 1 jar sour cherries • ½ jar maraschino cherries • 3 tablespoons whiskey • 1 tablespoon starch • 2–4 tablespoons sugar • 1 cup cream • 1 cup cottage cheese • 6 tablespoons whiskey-cream-liqueur • 1 bag of vanilla sugar • 2 tablespoons sugar • 2 stalks peppermint • 1 bag Chocolate Ornaments

PREPARATION: Put the sour cherries in a pot. Purée the maraschino cherries with a little syrup. Bring to boil together with the cherries. Stir whiskey with starch until smooth. Pour over the cherries and let thicken. If necessary, sweeten with a little sugar. Leave the mixture aside to cool. Whip the cream until stiff. Mix cottage cheese with liqueur, vanilla sugar and 2 tablespoons sugar until creamy. Stir in cream. Decoratively layer the sauce and stewed fruit in glasses and garnish with peppermint leaves and chocolate ornaments.

Ice Cream Sauce with Fruit Salad

INGREDIENTS: 2 tablespoons sugar • 1 tablespoon butter • 4 tablespoons oats • 2 oranges • 1 grapefruit • 1 apple • 2 kiwis • 1 cup strawberries • 2–3 tablespoons lemon juice • honey • 2 cups vanilla ice cream

PREPARATION: Melt the sugar into light caramel in a pan. Mix butter and oat flakes and roast for a short time. Let the roasted flakes cool down on a plate. Peel oranges and grapefruit carefully and cut them into bite-sized pieces. Wash the apple, quarter, pip it and cut it into segments. Peel kiwis and slice them into small pieces. Wash and halve or quarter the strawberries, depending on their size. Mix the fruit with lemon juice and a little honey. Melt the ice cream a little, add about 1 tablespoon honey and stir for a short time. Pour over the fruit salad and sprinkle the roasted flakes on top.

Marzipan Honey Sauce with Apple Peach Salad

INGREDIENTS: 2 apples • 3 peaches • juice of 1 lemon • 2 tablespoons honey • 3 ½ tablespoons marzipan • 1 cup cream • 4 tablespoons brandy • 5 tablespoons walnuts

PREPARATION: Wash and rub dry the apples and peaches. Halve, core, and cut all the fruit into small slices. Mix immediately with lemon juice and honey. Put the salad aside to cool. Grate marzipan coarsely and let it dissolve in the cream at low heat while stirring continuously. Pour in brandy and let the sauce cool. Chop the walnuts into pieces and roast them lightly in a frying pan without fat. Pour the lukewarm marzipan sauce over the salad and sprinkle walnuts on top.

Orange Mousse with Fruit Kebab

INGREDIENTS: 4 soft dried figs • ½ cup red port wine • 1 bay leaf • 1 apple • 1 pear • 2 nectarines • 4 tablespoons lemon juice • 4 big strawberries • 5 tablespoons butter • 5 tablespoons icing sugar • 1 package vanilla sugar • 2 tablespoons orange liquor • 1 untreated orange • 3 egg yolks • 2 egg whites • ½ cup Crème fraîche • 2–3 tablespoons orange-flower honey

PREPARATION: Prick figs all over with a wooden skewer and simmer in port wine with a bay leaf for 20 minutes. Wash quarter and core apple, pear and nectarines. Then slice. Drizzle with lemon juice immediately. Wash and clean strawberries. Skewer all fruits alternately on 4 skewers. Heat butter with icing sugar for 2 minutes, add vanilla sugar and liquor. Wash orange in hot water, peel the skin with a zester and add half of it to the butter mixture. Put skewers onto a baking tray and spread butter mix all over. Cook on a grill for 5 minutes. Squeeze the orange. Whisk egg whites with orange juice and remaining orange peel until creamy. Whisk the whites until stiff. Put yolk pastry cream in a dish with one ice cube and whisk until cool. Stir in Crème fraîche, honey and then mix in whisked whites. Pour orange mousse over fruit skewers.

TIP

The orange mousse is also delicious with exotic fruit skewers of pine, apple, mango, papaya, bananas and kiwis.

Orange Syrup with Summer Fruits

INGREDIENTS: 1 honeydew melon • 2 oranges • 1 cup strawberries • 7 tablespoons blue grapes • 7 tablespoons white grapes • 7 tablespoons pineapple cherry (Peruviana) • ½ bunch peppermint • 3 tablespoons orange liquor • 1 cup sugar • 1 tablespoon highly-concentrated vinegar • 2 pieces star anise • 5 spice cloves • 3 allspice berries • ½ cinnamon stalk

PREPARATION: Peel the melon and remove the seeds and fiber. Cut the melon into thin wedges. Peel 1 orange like an apple and cut in slices. Wash the strawberries and, depending on their size, halve or quarter them. Clean, halve and pit the grapes. Take the pineapple cherry out of the cover and wash. Wash the mint and pick leaves off the stems. Mix all the ingredients in a dish and drip liquor on them. Squeeze the second orange. Boil the juice slowly together with sugar, highly concentrated vinegar, anise, cloves and allspice berries. Then add the piece of cinnamon stalk and boil everything uncovered until it becomes syrupy. Put aside to cool, remove the solid spices and serve with the fruits.

Wine Mousse Sauce with Roasted Apples

INGREDIENTS: 3 ½ tablespoons chopped almonds • 4 russet apples • ½ cup Rum-Raisins • 4 tablespoons melted butter • 4 tablespoons crystal sugar • 2 eggs • 3 eggs yolks • ½ tablespoon meal starch • 1 pinch salt • 1 tablespoon lemon juice • 5 tablespoons sugar • 1 cup Vin Santo

PREPARATION: Roast almonds in a frying pan without fat and let them cool. Wash the apples and cut core out. Hollow out openings in the apples and save the apple scraps. Chop the scraps of apples and raisins coarsely and mix with almonds. Preheat the oven at 400°F. Fill the hollowed apples with the raisins-almonds-mixture and brush the outside with some melted butter. Put the apples in a baking dish and roast them in the oven for 25–35 minutes. Brush with the remaining butter and sprinkle with crystal sugar. Whisk 4 yolks (save the whites!) and 1 whole egg with starch, salt, lemon juice, sugar and Vin Santo in a double boiler until foamy. Whisk the egg white until stiff and stir in. Arrange the roasted apples onto dessert plates and pour some wine mousse over them.

TIP

For the wine mousse sauce, you can use white wine, dessert wine like Marsala or the favourite sherry. When using dessert wines, 3½ tablespoons sugar is enough.

Peach Liquor Yogurt Sauce for Nectarines

INGREDIENTS: 1 cup vanilla yogurt • 1 cup mascarpone cheese • 1 small package vanilla sugar • 5 tablespoons peach liquor • 1 package Citrus-flavored baking agent • 1 lime • 1 cup cream • 5 nectarines • 3 tablespoons sugar • 3 ½ oz grated milk chocolate • 1 package of chocolate garnish

PREPARATION: Mix the yogurt with mascarpone, vanilla sugar, 3 tablespoons liquor, Citrus-flavored baking agent and lime juice. Whip the cream until stiff and stir in. Wash, quarter and pit the nectarines. Cut one of them into thin slices, finely dice the remaining ones, drip liquor on the rest and mix with sugar. Let sit for 15 minutes. Alternately layer the liquor sauce in glasses with the nectarines and the grated chocolate. Garnish with nectarine slices and chocolate decoration.

Nougat Sauce with Farina Flammeri

INGREDIENTS: 3 cups milk • 2 cups cream • salt • 10 tablespoons hard-wheat semolina • 10 teaspoons sugar • 1 bag vanilla sugar • a bit grated lemon peel • 1 egg • 3 oz nougat • 2–3 tablespoons cooled coffee • ½ honeydew melon • 2 kiwis • 1 big peach • 4 oz grapes • 10 cocktail cherries • 1 tablespoon brandy • 1 tablespoon honey

TIP
If you want to make it quickly, use 1 bottle of chocolate dessert sauce instead of home-made chocolate sauce.

PREPARATION: Boil milk and 1 cup cream with a bit of salt. Sprinkle semolina in and, stirring continuously, simmer 3 minutes. Stir in sugar, vanilla sugar and lemon peel. Divide egg. Blend yolk with semolina. Whisk egg white until stiff and stir in cooled semolina. Rinse pudding mold with cold water and place semolina inside. Cool completely. Unmold on plate. Heat remaining cream with crushed nougat and coffee and stir until smooth. Cut small balls out of melon. Peel kiwis and peach and cut in small pieces. Clean and wash grapes. Mix all fruits with brandy and honey. Let sit 30 minutes. Pour nougat sauce over flammeri and serve with fruit salad.

Orange Sauce with Chocolate Pudding

INGREDIENTS: 3 ½ oz chocolate • 1 cup butter • ¾ cup sugar • 2 packages vanilla sugar • 3 eggs • 1 tablespoon rum • 1 teaspoon instant coffee • 7 tablespoons oats • 7 teaspoon starch • 1 tablespoon of cocoa • 2 teaspoons baking powder • 4 tablespoons milk • butter for the mold • 2 tablespoons crushed crispy oat flakes • 2 big oranges • ½ cup semi-dry white wine • 1 teaspoon butter • 1 cup cream

PREPARATION: Grate the chocolate finely. Stir butter with ½ cup sugar and 1 package vanilla sugar until foamy. Mix eggs, rum, coffee powder, oat flakes, 5 teaspoons starch, cocoa and baking powder. Add milk gradually. Grease a pudding mold, sprinkle with crushed oat flakes and pour in the mixture. Cover and cook in a double boiler for 75 minutes. Wash oranges in hot water peel the skin off and squeeze out the juice. Thicken remaining starch with wine and sugar. Stir in orange peel, juice, butter and let cool. Whisk the cream until stiff with the remaining vanilla sugar. Take the pudding out of the mold and serve with the sauce and whipped cream.

Banana Caramel Sauce with Pineapple Pancake

INGREDIENTS: 4 eggs • salt • a bit of grated orange peel
• 1 tablespoon maple syrup or sugar • 1 cup flour • 1 ½
1 ¾ cup milk • 1 big can pineapple rings • baking fat
• 4 teaspoon grated coconut • 5 tablespoons
sugar • 1 tablespoon honey • 1 cup cream
• 1 small, ripe banana • 2 tablespoons butter

PREPARATION: Mix the eggs with a pinch of salt,
orange peel, flour and maple syrup or sugar.
Pour 1½ cups milk gradually into it and stir until
smooth. Let the batter stand for 30 minutes. Add
more milk if necessary. Let the pineapple rings
drain well. Heat some fat in a pan and fill it with one quarter of the batter. Lay 3 pineapple rings on top and sprinkle
1 teaspoon of grated coconut on the surface. If necessary,
add some more fat to the pan, turn the pancake and bake
until done. Bake the other 3 pancakes in the same way.
Melt the sugar into light caramel. Heat honey and 1 cup
cream and pour carefully into the caramel. Peel the banana
and crush with a fork. Add to caramel and heat. Stir in butter and strain the mixture through a strainer. If desired, add
the remaining cream. Serve warm or cold with the pancakes.

> **TIP**
> It is best to keep the freshly made pancakes warm in the oven, heated at 212°F, until all the pancakes are done

Orange Chocolate Sauce with Sweet Chestnut Purée

INGREDIENTS: 1 lb peeled and boiled sweet chestnuts • 2 cups milk • gingerbread spice • a bit of grated lemon skin • 1 package vanilla sugar • 1 vanilla bean • 2–3 cups cream • 3 egg yolks • 2 tablespoons sugar • ¼ cup orange liquor • 1 tablespoon cocoa • 7 tablespoons Herren Chocolate (high contents of cocoa) • 1 tablespoon orange blossom honey

PREPARATION: Chop the sweet chestnuts coarsely and boil in the milk with a pinch of gingerbread spice until very soft and all the liquid boils away. Spice with grated lemon skin and vanilla sugar. Purée the sweet chestnuts and strain them with a fine strainer. Cut the vanilla bean open, scrape the pulp out and bring to a boil with the chestnuts and 1 cup cream. Stir the yolks with sugar until foamy. Add the cream slowly and stir at a low heat until mixture thickens. Remove the vanilla husk. Mix the cooled off cream with the sweet chestnut purée and a bit of orange liquor. Heat 1¼ cup cream with cocoa and chopped chocolate and stir until smooth. Mix with the remaining liquor, orange peel and honey. If desired, add more cream. Press the sweet chestnut purée through a potato masher and pour the sauce over it. Serve with whipped cream.

Kiwi Sauce with Peach Mousse

INGREDIENTS: 3 egg yolks • 6 tablespoons powdered sugar • 3 leaves gelatine • 1 small can peaches • 1 cup cream • 3 tablespoons peach liquor • 3 ripe kiwis • 1 tablespoon honey • 1 tablespoon lemon juice • 1 tablespoon peppermint liquor or peppermint syrup • 2 stalks peppermint

PREPARATION: Stir the yolks until foamy with sifted powdered sugar. Soak the gelatine in cold water. Drain the peaches and save the juice. Purée the peaches with a bit of juice and strain through a fine strainer. Take 1 cup of the pureed peaches and heat. Squeeze the gelatine out and dissolve in the warm purée. Stir in the yolk mixture. Whisk the cream until stiff and add it to the cooled purée. Season with peach liquor. Let the cream cool. Skin and purée the kiwis. Mix with honey, lemon juice and peppermint liquor or syrup. Cut gnocchi out of the mousse and serve with the sauce. Garnish with mint leaves.

TIP

It is also tasty the other way around: Kiwi mousse with peach sauce. Bring fresh kiwi purée to boil and thicken it with gelatine.

Tipsy Cherry Sauce with Poppy Seed Pie

INGREDIENTS: 1 lb cherries • ½ cup cherry spirit • 5 tbsp sugar • 1 cup cherry juice • 1 teaspoon starch • ½ lb frozen flaky pastry • 1 egg yolk • 2 tablespoons chopped almonds • 1 tablespoon sugar• 1 cup mascarpone cheese • 1 bag Poppy Seed-baking substance • 2 limes • ½ cup cream • 2 bags cherry-flavored baking agent

PREPARATION: Pierce cherries with toothpicks, pour cherry juice over them and let sit overnight. Add juice and sugar and boil. Stir starch in cold water until smooth. Mix with cherries, thicken once. Thaw pastry. Preheat oven to 400°F. Roll pastry and cut out 4 circles 3 in diameter. Put onto baking tray lined with baking paper. Cut 8 strips out of remaining pastry. Brush pastry pieces and strips with yolk and put 2 strips on top of each often on each circle. Brush with yolk and sprinkle with almonds and sugar. Bake 15–20 minutes. Press the hot pies down in the middle with spoon. Mix mascarpone with poppyseed filling. Wash 1 lime and rub dry. Grate peel and add to the poppyseed mixture. Squeeze fruit out. Stir juice and cherry-flavored baking agent with the poppyseed. Fold in whipped cream. Fill in pastry and serve with cherry sauce.

Nut Croquant Sauce with Roasted Bananas

INGREDIENTS: 3 ½ tablespoons walnuts • 7 tablespoons sugar • 2 tablespoons acacia honey • 1 cup cream • 1 small cup espresso • 4 bananas • 4 tablespoons lemon juice • 4 tablespoons butter • 4 portions vanilla ice cream • 2 stalks lemon grass

PREPARATION: Chop the walnuts coarsely. Melt sugar into light caramel. Mix about 2 tablespoons caramel with the nuts and allow it to stiffen on a plate. Heat honey with cream and espresso and com-

bine with the remaining caramel. Let the sauce cool a little. Peel the bananas, cut them lengthwise and drizzle with lemon juice. Heat butter in a pan and roast the bananas in it for about 5 minutes. Chop the nut mixture coarsely and mix with the sauce. Arrange the bananas onto plates, pour the sauce over and put 1 portion of vanilla ice cream on each plate. Garnish with lemon balm leaves.

Limoncello Sauce with Warm Fruit Salad

TIP

If you pour cooler liquid into caramel, the sugar becomes stiff. You must reheat it until the caramel has melted again.

INGREDIENTS: 5 tablespoons sugar • 4 tablespoons Limoncello (lemon liquor) • 6 tablespoons lime juice • 1 mandarin • 2 tablespoons butter • 1 mango • 1 papaya (pawpaw) • 1 banana • 1 pear • 1 peach • 2 tablespoons orange-flower honey • ½ cup Crème Fraîche Double • 6 lemon balm leaves

PREPARATION: Melt sugar into light caramel. Heat lemon liquor and citrus juices and pour into the caramel. Stir in butter. Preheat the oven to 400°F. Peel, pit and cut all the fruits into thin slices. Put the fruit into a heat-proof dish and pour the sauce over it. Bake in the hot oven for 10 minutes. Stir the fruits for a short time. Mix honey and Crème Double and pour over the fruit salad. Sprinkle with lemon balm leaves.

Egg Mousse with Poppy Seed Parfait

INGREDIENTS: 4 eggs • 3 egg yolks • 5 tablespoons sugar • 3 tablespoons poppy seed baking mix • 1 cup cream • 5 tablespoons powdered sugar • 1 bag of vanilla sugar • grated lemon peel • 1 pinch salt • 1 tablespoon orange liquor • 1 cup blackberries • 2 tablespoons blackberry liquor

PREPARATION: Stir 2 eggs and the egg yolks together with sugar in a double boiler until foamy. Add poppy seed baking mix and place the bowl in a bigger dish with ice water and ice cubes. Whip the cream until stiff and add to the poppy seed mixture. Pour into 4 cups or into a bigger mold and put in the refrigerator for at least 6 hours. Separate the remaining eggs. Whisk the egg yolks with sifted icing sugar and vanilla sugar until they are creamy. Flavor with lemon peel. Whisk the egg whites with a pinch of salt until stiff and add orange liquor to the yolk mixture. Drizzle the blackberries with blackberry liquor let and sit for a short time. Take the parfait out of the refrigerator 30 minutes before serving and garnish with egg mousse and marinated blackberries.

Goat Cheese Sauce with Gratinated Figs

INGREDIENTS: 6 big fresh figs • butter for baking molds • ½ cup red port wine • 1 small stalk rosemary • 5 tablespoons sugar • ½ cup mascarpone cheese • 3 ½ tablespoons goat cheese • 2 tablespoons acacia honey • 1 tablespoon lime juice • a little milk • freshly ground white pepper • 12 Amaretti (almond biscuits)

PREPARATION: Wash and rub the figs dry. Quarter 2 of them, cut the others crosswise and make a little hollow in the middle. Grease 4 small heat-proof molds and put one and half figs into each. Boil port wine with rosemary and sugar until mixture reaches a syrup-like consistency. Remove the rosemary and pour the syrup over the fruits. Mix mascarpone with goat cheese, honey, lime juice and  a little milk until creamy. Flavor very slightly with pepper. Put the mixture on the figs and bake in a hot oven for 2–3 minutes. Crush the Amaretti biscuits and sprinkle them over the dessert.

Grappa Grapes Sauce with Baked Camembert

INGREDIENTS: 5 oz white grapes • 5 oz blue grapes • 4 tablespoons wine or apple jelly • 5 tablespoons Grappa liquor • 4 halves Camembert • 2 tablespoons finely chopped walnuts • 8 tablespoons breadcrumbs • 2 eggs • salt • freshly ground pepper • fat for frying

PREPARATION: Clean all the grapes, wash them and let drip dry. Halve and core the grapes. Mix with jelly and Grappa liquor and let sit for at least 3 hours. Let the Camembert pieces sit at room temperature for 1 hour. Mix walnuts on a plate with breadcrumbs. On another plate, mix eggs with some salt and pepper. Heat a sufficient amount of fat in a pan.

> **TIP**
>
> Instead of Camembert, you can coat any other aromatic, medium soft cheese and fry it quickly.

Pull the Camembert pieces through egg first and then coat them with breadcrumbs. Fry the cheese until golden and let a kitchen paper towel absorb the extra fat. Decorate 1 baked Camembert with some Grappa Liquor-Grapes-Sauce.

Vanilla Sauce

INGREDIENTS: 2 beans vanilla • 2 cups milk • 6 egg yolks • 1 pinch salt • 7 tablespoons sugar

PREPARATION: Slice open the vanilla beans and scrape out the pulp. Add pulp and vanilla beans to milk and heat. Let sit for 10 minutes. Stir the egg yolks with salt and sugar in a bowl until creamy. Add the hot milk, poured through a strainer, to the mixture and whisk until thick in a double boiler.

Chocolate Sauce

INGREDIENTS: 3 ½ oz fine chocolate • 5 tablespoons cream • 1–2 teaspoon sugar • a little brandy • 3–4 tablespoons whipped cream

PREPARATION: Chop the chocolate coarsely and dissolve it in the cream over mild heat. Flavor with sugar and brandy and, when cooled, stir cream into it.

Marzipan Sauce

INGREDIENTS: 4 tablespoons chopped almonds • 3 oz marzipan • 1 cup cream • 1–3 tablespoons almond liquor • possibly some milk

PREPARATION: Roast the almonds slightly in a pan without fat. Cut the marzipan in small pieces and heat slowly with cream, stirring continuously. Mix with roasted almonds and liquor. You can dilute the cooled sauce with a little milk.

Caramel Sauce

INGREDIENTS: ½ cup of sugar • 3 tablespoons coffee • 1–2 tablespoons honey • 1 cup cream • a little milk

PREPARATION: Melt the sugar into light caramel. Heat coffee, honey, and cream and add slowly to carmel mixture. When cooled, dilute the sauce with a little milk.

Fresh Fruit Sauce

INGREDIENTS: 1 lb mixed berries • 2–3 tablespoons of icing sugar • strawberry liquor • raspberry liquor or anything similar of your choice

PREPARATION: Sort the fruits, wash or peel, core and cut in small pieces. Mix with sifted icing sugar and let the juice sit. Then purée it and, if desired, strain through a fine strainer. Flavor with some suitable liquor.

Tips

In this chapter, you will learn all that is worth knowing about sauces: how they are thickened, what you should do if something goes wrong and how sauces can be preserved. We will explain all the special terms and give you tips about which sauce goes best with which meal.

Sauce-Thickening

A sauce is not broth. A sauce is the finishing touch to any type of meal, ranging from salads to meat dishes, fish and sea food, potato and vegetable platters, rice and pasta dishes, and, of course, desserts. What would pork roast with dumplings be without thick, dark beer pesto? How would spaghetti taste without tomato sauce or Pesto? What is a salad without dressing? Roast beef without remoulade? And what do we miss in a fruit dessert? A heavenly smelling vanilla sauce.

Thicken with flour and starch: All sauces should be somewhat thick and the best agent for it is roux, which can taste milder or heavier or be lighter or darker. Hot or cold broth is poured over flour, browned in butter, until the sauce reaches the desired thickness. It is seasoned with spices, herbs, wine, etc. Meat juices have an especially good taste and a velvet consistency if thickened with buttery flour: a mixture of butter and flour in which butter and flour are kneaded together in a 1-to-1 ratio, put aside to cool and stirred bit by bit into the gravy.

Sauces thickened with flour must be cooked for 5 to 10 minutes or longer so that the floury taste disappears.

Sauces can also be thickened with starch from potatoes, corn meal or arrowroot flour. The starch should always be stirred in a little cold water until smooth. Then it is poured into a boiling liquid and the sauce is left to thicken.

There are light and dark sauce thickeners available in shops, which can easily be stirred into gravy. In contrast to various sauce products for roast beef, roast pork, roast minced meat or goulash, they are neutral in taste. They can even be stirred into water. Powder mixes for light sauces, such as Hollandaise Sauce and others, can be helpful in the kitchen.

THICKENING WITH BUTTER: Sauce base from roasted and braised meat can also be thickened with butter. Small pieces of ice-cold butter are thrown rather than stirred into a hot sauce base. The sauce gets lightly thickened and must be served immediately.

THICKENING WITH EGG YOLK: Light sauces for vegetable, fish, sea food and light (white) meat can be thickened nicely with egg yolk. Egg yolk is stirred in a bowl with some hot broth, sauce base or similar foundation and then poured into hot, but not boiling, liquid. To avoid the egg becoming lumpy, add a dash of salt to the mixture. The sauce is carefully heated until it reaches a desired consistency.

THICKENING WITH POTATOES AND VEGETABLES: Sauces for meat, fish, and vegetables can also be thickened with boiled vegetables, such as potatoes, carrots, or celery. You can later purée the vegetables in boiling or braising liquid. Boiled aspargus tastes striking with a sauce from asparagus stock, flavored with butter or cream and lemon juice.

EMERGENCY HELP

In spite of experience and adherence to recipe directions, it can happen that a sauce doesn't come out as we hoped. Several helpful tricks will help you ensure that you never have to leave out the sauce for a dish you have been preparing with care.

THE SAUCE IS TOO THIN: Simply let the sauce bubble uncovered for a few minutes until it reaches the desired consistency. Or you can thicken the sauce with a light or dark sauce thickener, such as flour stirred in cold water or stirred-in starch. You can also purée some boiled vegetables, such as potatoes, carrots, and onions.

THE SAUCE TASTES DULL: Let the sauce bubble uncovered for several minutes. As the remaining liquid evaporates, the sauce tastes stronger. Often it just needs a bit of salt and pepper to give it some flavor, but if something further seems lacking, a small stock cube is good for intensifying the taste. Or some fresh or dried herbs can be used. Herbs are also useful if the sauce gets burnt.

THE SAUCE GETS BURNT: There is no good solution here: the sauce is damaged and must be thrown away. As a quick substitute, sauce powder from a supermarket can be mixed with sweet or sour cream like Crème fraîche or sour cream and various spices and herbs. A new sauce can be composed of a little wine, a teaspoon of mustard, some tomato paste, a few thyme or rosemary leaves, a few dried mushrooms, some grated lemon peel, a bit of ginger, chili and good quality oil or a portion of butter.

THE SAUCE IS TOO THICK: A bit of red or white wine, sherry or port wine, some meat or vegetable stock, cream, some ready-made sauce or butter make your sauce thinner or more liquified. If your sauce is too strong in flavor, your solution is a bit of water. Dessert sauces can be thinned with milk, cream or liquor.

THE SAUCE HAS CURDLED: When a sauce with cream has gone lumpy, it might be due to too little fat contained in the cream or the sauce that has been boiled too violently. Sour cream with 10 % fat must not be boiled after being added to the finished sauce. Sour cream with about 24% fat, sweet cream with more than 30% fat, Crème fraîche, a lightly sour cream with over 35% fat, and Crème double, a very fatty, sweet cream with about 40% fat, are best for hot sauces.

Cheese sauce based on cream and grated cheese can get lumpy as well if the sauce is too hot. The famous Hollandaise sauce also has a tendency to curdle. It can often be helped by stirring an egg yolk and little water in a hot bath until creamy and gradually adding the curdled sauce. Mayonnaise can also get lumpy. When prepared from egg yolk and butter or oil, all the ingredients must have the same temperature; they can be combined only in small amounts and must never be boiled too much.

THE SAUCE IS TOO SALTY: The salty taste can be reduced by adding cream. For warm sauces, you can add grated potatoes while the sauce is boling. In cold sauces, the salty taste can be moderated by oil, juice, yogurt or other milky products. However, if you put a large amount of salt in the sauce, nothing can help to change the taste.

THE SAUCE GOES LUMPY: No chef is happy about lumps - big or small - in the sauce. Such sauce, sweet or hot, is strained through a fine strainer and the undesired lumps are gone.

THE SAUCE IS TOO FAT: Liquid fat can be removed with a spoon. This can very easily be done if you put the sauce in the refrigerator to cool down. The fat gets solid on the surface and can be easily removed. You can also put some ice cubes in a kitchen napkin and by carefully dipping them in the sauce, you bind the fat onto the ice. There are sauce pans available with two spouts: the fat flows through the upper spout and the fat-free sauce through the bottom one.

THERE ISN'T ENOUGH SAUCE: In this case, a nice portion of butter or sweet or sour cream or Crème fraîche is the solution. Then season the sauce once more. Other solutions include sauce products by Maggi or Knorr & Co. These ready-made sauce products can thin sauces down. In case you encounter the opposite problem, keep some stock in the freezer to make a bigger amount of sauce on the spur of the moment.

THE GRAVY IS TOO WHITE: There is a dark brown, neutral-tasting product which can tint pale gravy. A dark sauce thickener brings some color into the sauce.

WHITE SAUCES ARE COLORLESS: Sometimes a cook wants a white sauce to appear a little more striking on the plate. Egg yolk, paprika, tomato paste, saffron, and turmeric are suitable for adding appetizing color. A fresh green effect is produced with finely chopped herbs, such as parsley, chervil, basil, dill, etc.

SAUCE BASE OR STOCK IS CLOUDY: Usually gravy and stock from meat, poultry, and bones become cloudy if they are boiled too heavily. On the other hand, the good flavor is hidden in the lumpy part. Those of you who desire to have a clear liquid should pour the stock through a paper filter or stir two egg yolks in the liquid, boil for 3 to 5 minutes and let it sit for another 10 to 15 minutes on the side of the stove. Then remove the foam and pour the stock slowly through kitchen gauze.

You can buy ready-made sauces of various flavors. Such sauce base can be boiled down and used for both the thinning and improving the taste of your sauce.

THE DESSERT SAUCE IS TOO SWEET: Sauce which is too sweet can be saved by adding some unsweetened whipped cream and fruit sauce can be saved by adding unsweetened fruit purée from deep-frozen fruits. Or a bit of lemon or lime juice will help.

DRESSING OR MARINADE IS TOO SOUR: If salad sauce is too sour, remove several tablespoons of the sauce and stir in oil, cream, yogurt, juice, broth or wine with the remaining dressing. If necessary, put the removed sour sauce back into the sauce later. You can thin down a very sour marinade with wine or water. Sometimes, a little sugar will help neutralize the sour taste.

PRESERVING

Stocks and sauce bases can be frozen for up to 6 months. A strong sauce base can also be frozen in an ice tray. In this way, a small amount can easily be used to finish or thin down a sauce. Vegetable and fruit purées (Coulis) can also be frozen for several months. Gravies should, if possible, be frozen separately from meat. The containers should never be quite full.

Mayonnaise, remoulade, English Creme and Hollandaise sauce should not be frozen. Also, chutneys and relishes are not suitable for freezing. They can, nevertheless, be kept in airtight jars. Both the jars and lids must be clean. The ingredients must be put into jars while hot and immediately closed with a twist-off lid. Cold sauces, such as dressings, mayonnaise, dips, salsas etc., should be kept in the refrigerator no longer than 2 to 3 days. Boiled, sweet sauces can be stored in the refrigerator for up to 3 days.

Tip

At the table, you will best keep warm sauces warm with the help of a rechaud. Foamy whisked sauces cannot sit for a long time.

Kitchen lexicon

As everywhere, even in the kitchen, there are special terms which aren't understood by everyone. Therefore, we explain the most important expressions in the following.

Béchamel sauce: This is one of the most widely-known and most beloved white sauces. It consists of roux and browned flour poured over milk.

Chaudfroid: Light or dark Velouté from meat, poultry or fish can be colored with tomato purée (red), lobster butter (pink), puréed herbs (green) and refined with cream and strongly reduced sauce base (Demiglace, Jus).

CHUTNEY: This fruity complement to many Indian dishes consists mainly of crushed fruits which can be prepared boiled or raw. Depending on the ingredients, they taste salty, sour or sweet-and-sour. They can be either mild or terribly hot.

CONCASSÉE: A fruity preparation from fresh, skinned and cored tomatoes that are diced and braised for a short time in a little butter and/or olive oil until the liquids evaporate. For seasoning, use onions, garlic, salt, pepper, sugar, lemon juice, fresh chili or chili powder and, of course, herbs such as parsley, dill, basil, thyme, rosemary, marjoram, sage and tarragon.

COULIS: Purée from vegetable or fruits can be seasoned with all possible spices and herbs, including wine, stock or cream according to your taste. Fruit Coulis is a fine fruit purée refined by sugar with liquor and other spices. Coulis should never stand for a long time because it loses its fine taste. Coulis can be served warm or cold. You can also thicken sauces with Coulis.

DEMIGLACE: This is a reduced sauce base or reduced stock seasoned with herbs, spices or wine, and has a syrup-like consistancy. Small pieces of cold butter are stirred into it.

DRESSING: They accompany and dress salads of every kind. There are no limits to ingredients: dressing can contain fruits (apple dressing), cheese (Parmesan dressing for Caesar salad), herbs, hard boiled and chopped eggs, chopped nuts, capers, pickled cucumber or finely diced vegetables. They are thickened with cream, mayonnaise, oil and other milky products. They are seasoned with vinegar, lemon or lime juice.

Duxelles: Braise finely chopped onions and finely chopped mushrooms in butter until the liquid evaporates. Season with salt, pepper and, according to your taste, with chopped parsley or finely-chopped dill. Concentrated stock or spicy sauce bases are mixed with Duxelles into a fine sauce, with or without cream.

Fumet: Another name for fish sauce bases.

Meat stock: A sauce base from braised bones (base for meat sauce) or fishbones (fish sauce base, Fumet), all possible spices, herbs and vegetables boiled slowly in wine, water, or in a mixture of both and then cooked until partly evaporated. Often, bones chopped in small pieces are roasted and browned, doused with water/wine and boiled to get the base for the meat sauce. Due to recent, highly publisized problems in the meat industry, beef or veal bones are rarely available in shops. Stocks and sauce bases are often boiled for hours. Differences between sauce bases and stock have disappeared. Fish sauce base consists mainly of the fishbones and heads (without gills) of white fish. It should never be boiled for more than 20 to 30 minutes.

JUS: Very little thickened, but fat-free gravy boiled down with sauce base or stock until the right taste is reached.

MAYONNAISE: A classic French sauce from egg yolk and oil, seasoned with mustard, lemon juice, salt and pepper. If you like it less robust, stir some yogurt into the finished mayonnaise. It can also be seasoned with herbs and spices.

MOLE: A typical Mexican sauce, mixed from braised, dried chili peppers, spices, fruits, herbs and dark chocolate. This striking sauce is suitable for different dishes.

MOUSSELINE: A substantial sauce in which a few spoonfuls of whipped cream are stirred in at the end.

PESTO: An ideal sauce for spaghetti consists of fresh basil, garlic, roasted pine nuts, grated Parmesan cheese and olive oil, all cut in small pieces. Other versions use also different herbs, such as parsley, chervil or herb mixtures. Apart from pine nuts, you can also use almonds, hazelnuts, walnuts or peanuts. You can't leave out olive or nut oil and some grated hard cheese.

PISTOU: A French herb sauce from garlic, herbs, such as parsley, basil, chervil etc., grated Parmesan cheese and olive oil. Italians add a few roasted pine nuts and call it Pesto.

Raita: This sauce, based on yogurt, comes from India, where it is served with especially hot curry dishes. Raita can contain potatoes, eggplant, carrots, cucumber and herbs.

Reducing: Stock, a sauce base or a sauce is cooked in an uncovered pot until the taste is convincing or the sauce has reached a desired consistency. Or liquid is reduced to a thick syrup with sugar. Also, wine and spice can be boiled so long that there is a spicy reduction left which can be combined with gravy or some other liquid into a sauce.

Relish: A spicy preparation, mainly from vegetables. It can consist of raw or boiled ingredients. It tastes salty, sweet-and-sour, hot or mild. Similarly to raita and chutney, it comes from Indian cuisine.

Remoulade: A sort of mayonnaise spiced with pickled gherkins, capers, herbs and mustard. It is served cold, with sliced roast meat, meat jellies, cold fish and boiled eggs.

Roux: A French word for browned flour. Butter is melted, flour is stirred in and, according to taste and subsequent usage, more or less strongly cooked. The roux is poured over with water, stock, sauce base or milk. Simmer about 10 minutes to get rid of the floury taste.

SABAYON: A similar preparation as Zabaione, consisting of egg yolk, eggs, sugar and wine. It is prepared over a hot double boiler and must be served immediately. Sabayon can also be prepared with eggs, stock, vermouth and herbs. When preparing this, you should be careful that the temperature isn't too high or the egg will curdle.

VELOUTÉ: This is a velvety sauce consisting of roux poured over any kind of stock and wine or sherry.

VINAIGRETTE: This versatile and simple sauce consists of oil and vinegar in the 3:1 relation as well as salt and pepper. It can be completed with mustard, honey or thick juices, citrus peel, herbs, horseradish, garlic, chopped onions, truffles and chilies. Apart from olive oil, use neutral oil like sunflower, sprout, thistle and peanut oil. Or you can use intense nut oil. If you find the taste of nut oil too strong, mix it with the same amount of neutral oil. In addition to lighter and darker vinegar essence, there are vinegars in a wide range of flavors: red wine and white wine vinegar, sherry, balsamic, quince, raspberry, cherry, elder etc. The classical Vinaigrette, thanks to its variety, becomes an all-round sauce for cold roast meat and fish as well as seafood, for salads and vegetable dishes.

DOUBLE BOILER: Frothy wine sauces like Sabayon, Zabaione, Hollandaise Sauce, English Creme, etc. are stirred in an egg-beat kettle (a metal dish with a rounded bottom) and hung in a bigger pot with simmering, not boiling water. It must be continuously beaten either with a hand mixer or a wire whisk so that the egg doesn't curdle and the sauce becomes frothy.

ZABAIONE: A frothy Italian wine sauce from egg yolk, sugar and Marsala wine. The ingredients are whisked until frothy over a double boiler and must be served immediately.

PEELINGS (ZEST), PEELER: Very thin strips of untreated citrus fruits are used. You can peel off strips of the washed fruits with a peeler and cut them into the finest strips. You can get a fine peeling tool in a shop to remove the citrus peel easily. Larger amounts of peelings should be cooked for 2 to 3 minutes.

WHICH SAUCE GOES WITH WHICH MEAL?

A few suggestions as to which sauce goes best with which meal follows. Of course, this is all a matter of taste. Not everyone likes tomato sauce with stewed or roasted fish. Some like to eat mayonnaise only with French fries, but the others only eat mayonnaise with tomato salad. But what can you match raita with when there is no hot Indian curry dish on the table? Read on and find out!

CHUTNEYS: Spicy fruit sauces accompany grilled, roasted and stewed meat, poultry and fish. Cold roast meat and fish go well with fruity chutney. Chutney sauces are also tasty with rice dishes, as well as meat fondues.

DIPS· Many hot and mild, sweet-and-sour and salty, smooth and creamy dips go with meat fondue. Dips are a casual and popular alternative to heavy, meat-based meals. They enhance party food. Party guests dip chips, bread or a chopped vegetable into fancy sauces.

DARK SAUCES: They develop during long roasting and braising of pork, beef, lamb or goat meat. A sauce also darkens when browned with roux. Dark sauces are suitable with all kinds of roast meat.

FRUIT SAUCES: Warm and cold fruit sauces go well with vanilla or chocolate ice cream, puddings and flammeris.

VEGETABLE SAUCES: Finely puréed or natural vegetable sauces are suitable with pasta, rice and potatoes, as well as on meat rissoles, poached or braised filets of beef or pork, chicken or turkey breast as well as on fish and seafood.

WHITE SAUCES: They are mostly mild in taste and therefore go best with mild vegetable, such as asparagus, kohlrabi, peas, spinach or black salsify. They are also suitable refined with butter, cream, lemon or lime juice and added to meat, fish or sea food.

HOLLANDAISE SAUCE: This famous sauce from egg yolk and butter cannot be omitted, especially when serving asparagus. Seasoned with mustard and herbs, such as tarragon, pepper and citrus juices, it is also tasty with a plate of spring-fresh vegetables or with fine meat, fish and seafood.

YOGURT SAUCES: Most yogurt sauces are cold and they accompany all sorts of salads. In the Middle East, yogurt is also served with lamb dishes.

CHEESE SAUCE: The favorite cheese-cream-sauce goes with spaghetti or some other pasta. But of course it is also delicious with hot potatoes, boiled rice or vegetables, such as cauliflower, broccoli, asparagus, black salsify or kohlrabi.

GARLIC SAUCE: Every white or dark sauce, whether cold or warm, becomes aromatic when a few garlic cloves are added. Garlic fans say a garlic sauce is always suitable. It is tasty with pasta, rice, potatoes, Mediterranean vegetables, such as artichokes, eggplants, fennel, pumpkin, paprika husks, tomatoes, zucchini, as well as green beans, cucumbers and mushrooms.

HERB SAUCES: They are tasty warm or cold with white vegetables, such as asparagus, kohlrabi, cauliflower, but with zucchini, mushrooms, potatoes, rice and noodles as well. Clear herb sauces with stock or sauce base, oil or butter and strong herbs, such as thyme, rosemary, sage, oregano and marjoram go well with Tortelloni and roasted meat and fish as well as with grilled seafood. See also Pesto/Pistou.

MAYONNAISE AND REMOULADE: These fatty, but delicious, sauces are mainly used for salad dressings. Mayonnaise is seldom served in large amounts. Remoulade goes well with cold roast meat, cold fish and grilled seafood.

MARZIPAN SAUCE: A nutty marzipan sauce is tasty with warm and cold fruit salad and fruit skewers. It tastes good with chocolate pudding, stuffed or plain pancakes and roast apples.

PESTO AND PISTOU: The first one originates in Italy, the other in France. Pesto belongs to pasta, Pistou enriches nourishing vegetable soups. They are best suited for seasoning various herb sauces.

RAITA: Indian specialty based on fresh yogurt. In its country of origin, it is combined with very hot meat, fish or rice and curry dishes. Because it tastes fresh, it is also suitable with crispy bread, grilled meat, fish and seafood.

RELISH: Again an Indian specialty, consisting mainly of crushed vegetables, which goes well with meat fondue, roasted and grilled meat, fish and seafood. Sometimes also with bread and sausage.

RED WINE SAUCE: These strong sauces complement dark, braised meat as well as poultry.

Salsas: Hot and mild salsas enrich meat fondue. They are also tasty with rice dishes, grilled and roasted meat or fish and deep-fried vegetables.